Elizabeth,

Best wishes to you
as you complete your
Ph.D. and start your
career!

7 PRACTICAL STEPS

FOR

EXECUTIVE ASCENSION

THE AFRICAN AMERICAN VOID
AND HOW YOU CAN FILL IT

7 PRACTICAL STEPS

FOR

EXECUTIVE ASCENSION

THE AFRICAN AMERICAN VOID AND HOW YOU CAN FILL IT

JONATHAN ROBERTS, PH.D

SIMMS BOOKS PUBLISHING

Publishers Since 2012

Published By Simms Books Publishing

Jonesboro, GA

Copyright © Jonathan Roberts, 2015

Library of Congress Cataloging in Publication Data

Roberts, Ph.D, Jonathan

7 Practical Steps for Executive Ascension: The African American Void and How You Can Fill It

ISBN: 978-0-692-43215-0

Printed in the United States of America

Drafted from dissertation. ProQuest LLC. 789 East Eisenhower Parkway P.O. Box 1346 Ann Arbor, MI 48106 - 1346 UMI 3505939 Copyright 2012 by ProQuest LLC. UMI Number: 3505939 A Dissertation Presented in Partial Fulfillment Of the Requirements for the Degree Doctor of Philosophy Capella University March 2012

Edited by: Sabrina K. Leroe

Cover Design by Urias Brown, Michael Shield Studios-urias@michaelshieldstudio.com

"My people are destroyed for lack of knowledge"
– Hosea 4:6

DEDICATION

I dedicate this book and all the efforts that went into it…

to God, for keeping me;

to my wife, for understanding me;

to my mother, for teaching me to never give up;

to my daughters; smart, talented and beautiful, you're poised for greatness!

to my grandson, the smartest kid I know, a star in the making!

iv

ACKNOWLEDGMENTS

To the ten gentlemen who so willingly told me about their
journeys for me to share with others, thank you for your
candid responses and for staying the course. I also thank
my doctoral mentor, Dr. Katherine Dew, for her support
and guidance in completing my Ph.D program.

TABLE OF CONTENTS

FOREWORD

The pursuit of success for African American men has been described as a "game" that must be played in positioning themselves to take full advantage of academic and professional opportunities. However, in acknowledging this component of life as a "game", we must also understand that in games there will be winners and losers. I am often reminded of advice that a football coach shared with me about the importance of preparation over motivation. He would yell furiously in explaining that even the most motivated could not run through a brick wall, but through preparation you would be prepared to scale the wall. In this text, Dr. Roberts has provided a playbook that can be used to help prepare the next generation of African American men to assume the role of leadership.

Many scholars and intellectuals have long discussed and debated W.E.B. Dubois's framing of "How does it feel to be a problem" in Souls of Black Folk. As a black professional male with a range of professional and academic experiences, I have experienced the muted expressions by classmates and colleagues of being "the problem". It is quite a revelation to be engaged in a conversation about the ills of the world only to step outside of the conversation and recognize you are the main character in the story. The story may involve themes of crime, uneducated, unemployed, irresponsible or lazy. While the themes may be a negative portrayal of what is wrong in society, the proposed main character may be singular in nature, African American men.

How do we begin and continue to push against a public narrative that decreases the value of African American men in the home, in the community, in the workplace and in society? It is imperative that a new story is told. The public discourse of African American men is not a homogenous story that is only told through our interaction with the justice system, it is not only told through our exploits in the sports arena and it is not limited to our ability to entertain the public. As Dr. Roberts explores the challenges of African American men in corporate America, he provides a learning tool that can help to unravel the negative public narrative and contrast it with examples of corporate success and resilience from African American men.

While highlighting the importance of building networks, relationships and identifying strong mentors as a tool for reaching professional success, this books furthers the need for a broader conversation on how do we engage African American males in ways that will transfer the knowledge of those who have traveled the paths of "hard knocks", "lessons learned" and "this is the right way". The idea of knowledge transfer through storytelling has a long and storied historical tradition in American society. Translating the stories of successful African American men is important for future and current professional men navigating through life. In my own personal reflection, the value of the informal sharing of personal and professional experiences of African American men in my life has been pivotal to my success thus far. While we can draw from the stories and experiences of these men, the academic rigor used to extract these stories encourages the application of these findings across a spectrum of organizational and community settings. Unlocking the keys of diversity can be challenging in many settings including government, academia, non-profits and for-profit organizations. Additionally, unlocking this issue as it relates to African American men is critically important.

As a story is always best told through the voices of the main characters, here we are presented with the realness and unique experiences of African American men on their journey to professional success. This story provides an insider's account of the strategic roadmap needed to ascend the corporate ladder. More importantly, we are provided with an alternate ending to an all too common negative narrative about African American men. In this version of the story, African American men are given the guide to ink their own story of success.

Corey Wiggins, MSPH, PhD

Jackson, MS

PREFACE

The road to success is always fraught with difficulties and struggles, especially in an African American man's journey upwards in the business world in the United States. While much has improved for people of color since the civil rights movement, today they still often face disadvantages in the workplace that prevent the full realization of their potentials – while African Americans account for 13% of the total population of the U.S. today, only 1.9% of senior management positions are occupied by African American men.

The statistics may seem all gloom and doom, but failure need not be the only fate. Many have succeeded, and I hope this book will shed light on how you can achieve it too.

This is actually an opportune time for a closer look at executive ascension and succession planning. If research is correct, by 2015, minorities will represent 33 % of the total United States population (Barney, 2002), and the population of European Americans will accordingly decline by 8.1 % from 2000 to 2020 (Bureau of Labor and Statistics, n.d.). This will result in voids in *Fortune* 1000 management structures, which up to this time have been largely dominated by white men, and capable candidates will be needed to fill the talent pipeline. African American men represent a viable group to fill the talent void because they are skilled and underrepresented in *Fortune* 1000 senior management positions.

This book is based on my doctoral research, and a culmination of years of academic study and research.

Accordingly, in the book I drew on academic publications in my analysis and explanation of the underrepresentation of African American men in executive positions. And to provide solutions for this problem, I interviewed ten African American men who have succeeded in their journey to the executive suite. Their stories, I hope, will be a source of inspiration for the readers, and the seven tips extracted from their experiences will serve as a roadmap to corporate ascension for aspiring professionals.

An African American man myself, I have worked in American corporations for the past 25 years. Now 50 years old, I have worked for five *Fortune* 500 companies, and attained the level of Customer Vice President in my most recent organization. I have been an active participant in the succession-planning and talent-management process, and I have participated on both sides of the desk, evaluating employees or being evaluated in the succession-planning process. I have relocated 14 times and I have lived in every region of the United States.

During my time in the corporate world, I have experienced many of the issues described by the interviewees in this book. I can recount the times that I was passed over for a promotion without given a good reason, or times that I was in competition with white women for the same job while I was clearly the stronger candidate. As I ascended on the corporate ladder, I also gained a birds-eye view of behind-the-scene decisions on succession planning and the mistakes that were made. However, for this research I was very careful to not let my personal experiences or opinions seep into the discussion or analysis of the research.

As a conscious effort to not let my personal opinions or views distract the message of the interviewees, I follow A. Giorgi's guidance on the need to bracket my thoughts and experiences as the researcher to prevent bias, and to validate the essence of the phenomena of succession planning and talent management as perceived by African American men.

The subject of this book is of significant importance, because the opportunities to succeed in American corporations are bountiful, but not always revealed to African American men. It is my hope that this book will shed light on what contributed to the success of the interviewees in this book, and, consequently, point the way to executive ascension for African American men.

This book is also written for organizations as a whole and those who currently occupy the chair in the executive suite. As our workforce is shrinking in size and aging at the same time, it is more important now than ever for business leaders to consider a paradigm shift in their succession planning – specifically, by recognizing and training talented African American men, who remain underrepresented in senior management positions today. Perspectives shared in the following pages hopefully will provide corporations another lens to view diverse talent, which will broaden their talent pool and develop the next generation of leaders.

As will be evident in the following pages, it is only when diversity in management positions is achieved that diversity in the workplace can be ensured also. And only then can an organization's succession pipeline be appropriately replenished and its future success secured.

Jonathan Roberts, Ph.D.
April, 2015

PART I

AFRICAN AMERICAN MEN
IN EXECUTIVE SUITES:

THE VOID

CHAPTER 1

Landscape of Today's Corporate America

What is the secret to the success of a corporation? The answer is manifold and worthy of an entire library of treatises. Of the numerous factors that determine the success or failure of a company, in this book I focus on succession planning.

Part 1 of the book will form the framework of our investigation into the issue of succession planning. Chapter 1 will shed light on the current succession planning practices, and Chapter 2 gives an overview of the factors influencing those practices and resulting in the gaps in those practices (i.e. underrepresentation of African American men). In Part 2, I will move on to discuss how the gaps in current succession planning practices may be filled. Particularly, Chapter 3 reports the success stories of those who have attained senior management positions. Chapter 4 is a synthesis of the themes that emerged from the ten executives who shared their success stories, which give us the 7 tips for success. In Chapter 5, I list other tips and advice for those men of color who aspire to lead in the business world.

Succession Planning

Effective succession planning hinges on an organization's ability to prepare and develop talent to replenish the succession pipeline. Some of the most significant challenges faced by organizations have always been attracting, engaging, and retaining the right people with the right skills and capabilities to fill qualified and essential positions. As employees become older and more diverse, talent-management and subsequent succession-planning strategies become increasingly critical for organizations to understand and implement.

For organizations to be effective in their succession-planning processes, hiring managers need to look beyond their current source of candidates, Peter Cheese, former chairman of the Institute of Leadership and Management, observes that the new workforce is acquiring new skills as the current workforce is aging, and in this process of changing workforce, an organization must adjust its talent-management practices to maintain relevance.

In the 21st century, the practice of implementing succession plans will become more difficult for three reasons directly linked to demographic changes, notes Thomas Calo, Professor of Management & Marketing at Salisbury University. First, baby boomers have aged and are now entering their retirement years. Second, the effect of corporations reducing the size of their workforce for the last two decades reduced the availability of talent at the executive level. Lastly, the aging of the current workforce, coupled with the available pool of collegiate talent, will not provide enough employees to fill available jobs. Given these three reasons, Dr. Calo predicted that corporate America would face a talent shortage beginning in 2008 and extending until 2020 unless knowledge transfer plans are enacted (2008).

With the impending talent shortage, organizations will be even more pressed to find qualified candidates for the executive positions. Meyers and Dreachslin (2007) indicated:

> By 2050 veterans' knowledge and roles will be transferred to workers who do not look like them, and representation in the talent pool will increase by approximately 148 percent for Asians, 139 percent for Hispanics, and 58 percent for African Americans. (p. 290)

The talent shortage will force organizations to now focus on groups they have not widely developed in the past. Of particular concern is the lack of diversity within *Fortune* 1000 senior management structures, as African American men represent 1.9% of all senior management jobs (Bureau of Labor and Statistics, n.d.). African American men represent a group of employees who are underrepresented in the executive suite and their skills and availability present a long-term solution to abating the talent shortage.

Succession planning begins with having the appropriate talent identified to enter the succession pipeline. Altman (2009) determined the process needs to start early; otherwise the best talent will look for opportunities elsewhere. Ten years after the publication of McKinsey's (1997) study, *The War for Talent,* Guthridge, Komm, and Lawson (2008) reviewed the data and found one-third of organizations have not completed the necessary tasks to effectively manage the talent within their respective organizations. To manage talent successfully, executives must recognize their talent strategies cannot focus solely on the top performers; different things make people of different genders, ages, and nationalities want to work for a company (Guthridge et al., 2008). If talent strategies such as succession plans continue to focus on one gender or race, then the shortage of talented people will cause an organization to fail in producing the next generation of senior management. For the succession pipeline to be effective leaders must recognize the needs of the organization from diverse resources as opposed to the status quo.

The First Black CEO and His Successors

Effective usage of succession-planning strategies involves the highest level of the organization–the CEO (Berchelman, 2005). The number of African Americans who have reached the CEO level is considerably less than their European American counterparts. Jones and Wofford (1983) compared the characteristics among white CEOs to develop a concept of a Black CEO and to determine when an African American would be ready to lead a *Fortune* 500 company and chose 1999 as the target date. Indeed, the first African American to lead a *Fortune* 500 company was announced in 1999 with Franklin D. Raines becoming the CEO of Fannie Mae Corporation.

Although Raines cracked the glass ceiling for African American men, he experienced limited success and exited Fannie Mae unceremoniously. The eventual number of African American CEOs (all men) rose to 7, but as of this writing, there are only 3 African American CEOs (Byrnes, Crockett, and McGregor, 2009). As the leaders of the organization, CEOs provide the tone and direction for other leaders to follow (Davidson, Ning, Rakowski, and Elsaid,

2008). The lack of African American men in talent-management programs and the succession-planning process may be directly linked to the sparse number of current African American CEOs.

The impending labor shortage could introduce new opportunities for African American men. Berchelmen (2005) predicted, "Key positions will open at the same time statistically fewer people are available to fill the open jobs" (p. 12). However, with only 3 African American men being counted amongst *Fortune* 1000 CEOs, the statistics are not impressive (Byrnes, et al., 2009). With the labor pool declining, succession decisions could be further centered towards non-African Americans because of aversive racism, which Buttner, Lowe, and Billings-Harris, (2007) described as a —Modern form of prejudice that characterizes the racial attitude of many Whites who endorse egalitarian values and regard themselves as non-prejudiced, but who discriminate in subtle ways‖ (p. 130). The opportunities for African American men could be further reduced when aversive racism is coupled with system justification theory. Jost and Banaji, (as cited by Kay, Gaucher, Peach, Laurin, Friesen, Zanna and Spencer, 2009) stated, "The system justification theory is where people are motivated to defend and legitimize the systems in which they operate—that is, the rules and sociopolitical institutions within which people function" (p. 422). The system justification theory is applicable to this study because European American men may believe only they are capable of accomplishing goals or leading the organization and their thinking can sway who does and does not participate in the succession-planning process.

System justification theory has direct application to how succession decisions have been conducted in the past, resulting in an adverse effect on African American men. Peterson, Philpot, and O'Shaughnessy (2007) indicated African American men are third in the pecking order of corporate structures, after white men and white women. If companies continue to focus only on White men for senior management positions and ignore the talent crisis, then organizations can be exposed to greater risk of not having qualified talent for senior management positions.

By 2015, racial and ethnic minorities will make up one-third of the United States population, so the work that encourages and strengthens inclusive and diverse practices must be underway now (Barney, 2002). Census data further supports Barneys' view as the minority population has continued to increase since 1995 with minorities projected to be 33% of the U.S. population by 2015 and 47% by 2050 (United States Department of Commerce 1999, September). Considering the looming talent shortage, logic would suggest the shortage could be offset by the effective management of all talent. Specific consideration to diversity initiatives, with a particular focus on African American men, could provide one part of the solution to the talent shortage concern.

Senior management shortages are not going to improve and will only get worse. When organizations lose focus on developing their people the future of the organization can be at risk, as discussed by Ready and Conger (2003)

> The head of IBM GEOC, Tanya Clemons
> explains it this way: During the tough

economic conditions in the mid to late 1980s, we abandoned our commitment to leadership development and paid a dear price for that in loss of market leadership later on. We had to relearn the hard way the critical importance of grooming leaders at every level of this company and in every location around the globe in which we do business. (pp. 87-88)

In the current economic environment history could very well repeat itself and the mistakes of the 1980s could be replicated. The talent shortage could worsen and organizations will be challenged to find qualified candidates to backfill open positions. Many organizations are now accelerating spending on HR, training and workforce development, but most are still far away from having fully integrated talent-management processes and the capabilities needed to respond to the wider challenges of talent shortfall and competition (Cheese, 2008). Reilly (2008) believed human resources should take a more active role in the development of talent management and perform risk assessments to determine areas that are vulnerable within the organization, which will allow for more flexibility when the organization is challenged.

Not only are African American men underrepresented but they are also underrepresented at a time of looming talent shortages for senior management positions. Within the collection of *Fortune* 1000 CEOs only 3 African American men were counted amongst the group (Byrnes, et. al 2009). The faces of CEOs within *Fortune* 1000 companies primarily represent European American men with less than 1% of CEOs being African American men. According to government census data the African American population represents just fewer than 13% of the United States total population with a relative even distribution between men and women. Regarding senior management positions African American men represent 1.9% of the senior management population (see Table 1).

Clearly, the number of African American men in senior management positions does not equate to the population of African American men. The underrepresentation phenomenon is not limited to one particular industry but across the corporate landscape. As an example, Martin (2005) reviewed sales positions and noted African Americans represented less than 5% of sales people and they faced significant difficulties reaching middle and senior management positions. Meyers and Dreachslin (2007) acknowledged by 2050 overall White employees will decrease by 4% while African Americans will increase by 58% and in the healthcare field the disparity of African American employees is problematic. Focusing on African American men will provide organizations strategies they can employ to take advantage of a growing demographic, and enable the improvement of talent-management strategies and facilitate pipeline fill for senior management positions.

Table 1. Men Senior Management Participation Rate (reproduced from The U.S. Equal Employment Opportunity Commission, 2007)

Group	Total Employment	Senior Managers	Participation Rate
All Employees	50,188,492	901,484	100.00%
White Men	17,474,900	570,228	63.25%
Black Men	3,193,397	17,045	1.89%
Hispanic Men	3,960,529	27,358	3.03%
Asian Men	1,339,482	24,071	2.67%

The effects of the glass ceiling that hindered women have also hindered African American men. In 1991 the U. S. Congress enacted The Glass Ceiling Act in recognition of the inequities experienced by women and minorities in the workplace.

The intent of the Glass Ceiling Act was to eliminate disparate treatment experienced by women and minorities. In 1995 the Federal Glass Ceiling Commission discovered less than 5% of women held senior management positions and only two women held the CEO position (McDonald & Hite, 1998). The figures for women in 1995 are very similar to the current statistics of African American men.

The lack of African American men's exposure to talent-management and succession-planning programs could indicate a reason for the low representation at senior management levels. By understanding African American men' perceptions of the talent-management and succession-planning process, the men themselves can have more successful careers in executive ascension and organizations can have better strategies for talent-management and succession-planning processes for African Americans.

Research Method & Design

In order to understand the obstacles that African American men commonly face in their upward journey in the corporate world, I chose a qualitative research method that allowed me to interview successful African American men who have occupied senior management positions.

Whereas quantitative methods often use mathematical measure, qualitative studies focus on meanings or interpretations. This approach was chosen because, as Rizq and Target (2007) noted, "qualitative research has been considered particularly appropriate where the field of study is characterized by complexity, ambiguity, and lack of prior theory and research" (p. 133). Qualitative method gave me the freedom to explore the gap of knowledge about how African American men experience talent-management and succession-planning programs.

My research was a particular subtype of qualitative research method: phenomenology design. It explores what happened and how the phenomenon was experienced, a method that afforded me the space to focus on the lived experiences and subject perceptions of individuals, namely, African American men who successfully obtained executive positions.

This study focused on executives who are African American men, and explored their lived experiences and perceptions of the administration of talent- management and succession-planning programs. After a careful selection process that included a set of criteria, a sample of 10 executives was chosen. Their ages range from 35 to 70 years old, and were all either actively or had been employed in *Fortune* 1000 companies with at least the title of director in their position. The criterion of a director-level attainment was of particular importance, because at the director level, the participants have entered the succession-planning process. Other criteria included possession of a graduate degree, employment experience of 15 or more years, and experience with the succession-planning process.

These ten executives graciously responded to my written invitation to structured interviews and questionnaires. The results of the interviews, lasting 45 to 105 minutes, were collected, analyzed, and interpreted according to rigorous research protocols.

This study was conducted in compliance with the Capella University and the Institutional Review Board guidelines. All interviewee's express consent to participate in this study was obtained and confidentiality of their identity is strictly protected. No employee from the researcher's organization was used in this study. The interview questions were consistent for each participant, and I did not inject my own thoughts or sway the participant to respond in any specific or nonspecific manner. The actual interviews were conducted in private locations and ample time was allotted to each individual to fully answer the questions. All data was captured through a recording device or through written collection; and I am the only person who has access to participants' data, as all pertinent files are locked in my home office file cabinets.

CHAPTER 2

Factors Limiting Executive Ascension for African American Men

Some research has been done to explore the African American void in senior-level management positions. This chapter will summarize some of the findings regarding the factors limiting the executive ascension of African American men: (1) the upper echelon theory, (2) the obscure process of filling senior management positions, (3) inadequate workplace diversity, (4) insufficient talent management, and (5) lack of succession planning.

A conceptual diagram (see Figure 1 on next page) has been developed to connect the relationships of each component. The branch of ascension begins with talent-management and succession-planning programs. However, the base of the ascension is focused on senior management teams' theoretical practices along with their beliefs in diversity. To understand senior management teams, the upper echelon theory is reviewed to determine how organizations make decisions.

Limiting Factor #1: Upper Echelon Theory

In their studies on business management, Hambrick and Mason (1984) found several characteristics of top management and synthesized their findings into what is called *the upper echelon theory.* In a nutshell, upper echelon theory purports that "organizational outcomes, strategic choices and performance levels…are partially

predicted by managerial background and characteristics"
(p. 193). Confirmed by anecdotes and social science
studies, the upper echelon theory essentially is built on the
premise that senior executives' experiences, values, and
personalities influence their management, and
consequently, organizations actually become reflections of
their senior executives.

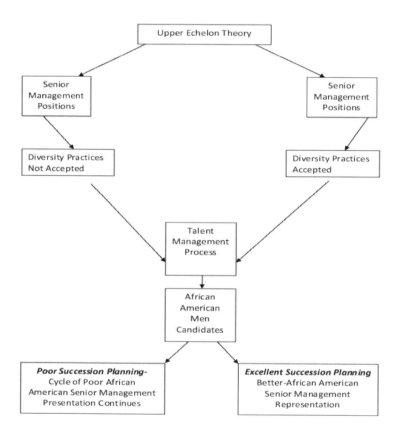

Image 1. Conceptual Diagram.

As an example, Hambrick and Mason (1984) noted in their upper echelon theory study that the executives of major firms they surveyed were white men, many of whom shared similar backgrounds: graduates of the same universities, members of the Protestant church, Republicans, and natives of the Midwest.

In plainer language, upper echelon theory explains the homogeneity that is pervasive in today's corporate America, where senior management positions are predominantly filled by white men. As senior managers make business choices, including promotions and/or talent management of employees, their own background and values influence their decisions. The result is often described as "mirror image," where succession planning is unduly influenced by favoritism and politics by how closely the new appointee mirrors the hiring manager (Hammett, 2008).

Hambrick and Mason asked the key question, "Why do organizations act the way they do?" (p. 193). Specific to the purposes of our discussions here, it may be more apropos to ask why corporations promote the people they do. In fact, the subject of this book and my doctoral research is understanding the perceptions of succession planning with African American men, building on the work of Hambrick and Mason (1984). Hambrick and Mason identified three benefits that can be obtained from understanding this issue:

> For the scholar, it may offer substantially
> greater power to predict organizational
> outcomes than current theories afford, a
> second benefit may come to those

responsible for selecting and developing upper level executives. For example, light may be shed on the tendencies of organizations led by older executives, those with formal management education, or those whose dominant career emphasis has been in a particular functional area. The effect of, say, management teams with long term, stable membership, as opposed to teams with short-lived membership, also may become more apparent, a third benefit may accrue to the strategist who is trying to predict a competitor's moves and countermoves. (p. 194)

The second benefit of selecting and developing the upper level executives is core to this book. Though Hambrick and Mason used the example of the selection process, focusing on older versus younger employees, I used the example of race factoring into the appointment equation. Understanding how organizations build their employee pipelines for selecting senior management can be critical in understanding the reasons for gaps in other areas of the executive population. If organizations are found to solely make decisions on age, or education, then the plausibility of equality is higher, but if there are other reasons such as racial identity, then the playing field may not be equal.

Hambrick and Mason (1984) also introduced a perceptual process that, if administered, is problematic and may present insight to the reasons why African American men are not better represented at the senior management level.

16

The perceptual process acknowledged three areas (a) a management team cannot scan every aspect of the company environment, (b) the managers' perceptions are limited because they perceive only the phenomena in their view, and (c) the bits of information chosen are filtered by the individuals' cognitive base and values. All three points provide solid indications of why African American men are not proportionally represented within organizations because hiring managers will say they cannot scan or recognize all employees, their perceptions of talent are limited to the group they are familiar with, which is typically fellow white men, and the filtering process allows them to see what they want to see.

Better still, Taylor (2004) explains, "Since white men hold the majority of Senior Leadership positions in corporate America, it is often that other white men are treated as members within the organizational *in-group* while people of color and women are viewed as *out-group* members" (p. 13). Granted, the management team cannot be privy of every aspect of an organization, but the recognition of in-group shortfall enables the organization to enact measures to target specific areas of the organization. If the organization deems African American men representation at senior levels of the organization important, then appropriate measures can be enacted and senior management can be required to comply.

Gaining management compliance addresses the second perceptual process as well. If the manager is limited by his field of vision, then by redirecting his eyesight better results can be attained. The third perceptual process is also problematic as it suggests the managers' filters are based upon their cognitive base and values. When the managers' filters are adjusted, the chances of African American men are improved when intervention from senior management includes them in the in-group.

Homogeneity vs. Heterogeneity in the Workplace

Hambrick and Mason (1984) also discussed the difference between heterogeneity and homogeneity that impacts an organization's structure, which concerns how similar or dissimilar the construct of the team is. In a heterogeneous team (Filley, House, and Kerr, 1976), the members tend to think differently, act differently and solve problems differently; this type of trait is effective for a team solving ill-defined problems. However, a homogenous group best manages routine problem solving. With the heterogeneous mode of thinking, the decision process of senior management to consider African American men for senior opportunities becomes an opportunity.

Although mirror image is often found in business decisions, which results in homogeneity in leadership positions and in organization management, those who are in management positions would do well to know that studies have cited many reasons to avoid homogeneity in the leadership. Specifically, Dowsett (2007) identified several features that result from homogeneity and cause once-successful companies to lose focus: denial, arrogance, and complacency.

Commenting on homogeneity versus heterogeneity in their discussion on the upper echelon theory, Pitcher and Smith

(2001) stated, "The heterogeneity of leadership teams can deliver a more complete analysis and search of strategic alternatives and exhibit greater creativity due to the exchange of diverse ideas" (p. 2). In the homogeneous team, all of the members think the same, act the same, and behave the same, which tend to lead to unchallenged decisions. Conversely, in heterogeneous groups, members of the group are challenged to maintain a respectful rapport and to consider their decisions more critically as a result of their differences. The heterogeneous team construct provides more diversity in the organization, leading to a more robust leadership.

Further, Hambrick and Mason (1984) believed, "In a turbulent environment, team heterogeneity will be positively associated with profitability" (p. 201). Morrison et al. (2008) also agreed, "Many organizations in the private sector have recognized that diversity contributes to the bottom line by enhancing the likelihood of arriving at better decisions to remain competitive in a global economy" (p. 79).

Although benefits abound for a heterogeneous environment, diversity remains a challenge. Morrison et al. offered the following five indicators for diversity within an organization

> [a] Diversity among the highest salaried employees in the organization, [b] number of individuals from culturally diverse backgrounds promoted, [c] number of new hires with diverse ethnic backgrounds, [e] diversity of both officers and members on a

board of directors, and [f] degree leaders are members in ethnic American professional organizations. (p. 79)

Measuring its diversity using these five indicators can help a senior management team to propel itself into a stronger position to better serve the organization. Employing a diverse team will enable organizations to develop products for a broader base of consumers, rather than a select few.

Limiting Factor #2: Obscure Process of Filling Senior Management Positions

The titles of senior management has been most commonly extended to the Chief Executive Officer (CEO), Chief Financial Officer (CFO), Chief Marketing Officer (CMO), Chief Operating Officer (COO) Chief Information Officer (CIO), Chief Sales Officer (CSO), Chief Technical Officer (CTO) and the Chief Diversity Officer (CDO). The decision to appoint an individual to a senior role does not rest with one person. Rather, many people are consulted and the paths for senior roles are divergent. However, the mechanism of this selection process is obscure to many. In line with Hambrick and Mason's upper echelon theory, senior management positions may be limited to a certain few, in accordance with managerial background and values.

To understand exactly what senior management means, we can look at Morrison's (2008) helpful description, characterizing "senior management" as

those professionals at the highest level of organization, such as the president, vice-president and treasurer. They are typically those administrators who provide the leadership for setting the standards for others to follow when addressing issues related to workforce diversity. It is their values, convictions, and concerns for others that reflect upon how serious workforce diversity issues are attended to as daily operations are carried out. (p. 79)

The current literature on senior management appointments and succession decision making is limited. However, anecdotal accounts are plentiful that reflect the mystery of the selection process. As such, the perception of African American men's succession-planning experience is a focal point of my research and this book. When most people perceive the succession-planning process to be shrouded in mystery and the secret is in the hands of only a select few (likely those who are similar to current senior management personnel), it is no wonder that African American men's representation in the executive suite remains awfully low. In order to fill the African American void in senior-level management positions, aspiring professionals must understand how the process works.

As an example, I will discuss the succession planning process specifically for one of the most critical positions in an organization – the CEO.

A CEO is a leader of the organization and accountable to the Chairman of the Board, the Board of Directors, and shareholders. In some cases the CEO can also be the Chairman of the Board, which adds complexity to the leadership relationship. The succeeding CEO is also chosen by the Board of Directors and is often recommended by his predecessor. If an organization does not have a successor in-house, it will conduct an outside search to fill the open post.

There are several reasons why a CEO's position becomes available in an organization. According to Comte and Mihal (1990), the decision to replace a CEO can stem from "external factors like environmental volatility, resource scarcity, and financial risk, along with internal factors such as size of the firm, characteristics of the board and power of the incumbent" (p. 47). Comte and Mihal believed that an external search for a CEO successor speaks to poor planning or the need to change the direction of the organization. In some cases, an outside senior manager at the CFO or COO level may be brought into the organization in a comparable role to enable the timing needed for the new leader to comprehend the company strategy and operations, and then the leader is eventually thrust into the CEO position.

Qualifications to become a CEO comprise a host of credentials, to include education, pedigree, experience, and knowledge. Cullinan (2008) commented, "CEOs can come from many backgrounds including marketing, accounting/finance, technical/scientific, and general administration, yet there is limited information in the literature regarding why companies choose CEOs with particular functional backgrounds and experiences" (p. 195). The selection of the CEO can be swayed by the industry in that the organization competes. As an example,

Cullinan discovered firms hiring marketing executives as the CEO were more likely to be in the retail sector, which enabled the organization to focus on higher gross profits and niche strategies.

The selection of the CEO will also have a direct impact on the organization's diverse practices based upon their past experiences and beliefs. If the CEO believes in diversity, then the application of diverse principles is more evident in the organization. Professionals who aspire to CEO-level positions should be attentive to succession-planning practices and business objectives of their organizations, and prepare themselves accordingly to be a qualified internal candidate.

Limiting Factor #3: Inadequate Workplace Diversity

The origins of diversity in the U.S., according to McVittie, McKinlay and Widdicombe (2008), "can be traced back to the USA in the mid-1980s (Thomas, 1986) and diversity in employment is seen as comprising the recruitment, retention, promotion and rewarding of a heterogeneous mix of individuals within an organization" (p. 349). Bell and Hartman (2007) added, "Few words in the current American lexicon are as ubiquitous and ostensibly uplifting as diversity. The actual meanings and functions of the term, however, are difficult to pinpoint" (p. 895). Kearney, Gebert, and Voelpel (2009) specified, "Despite significant gains in knowledge regarding the effects of different dimensions of diversity and of mean levels of personality variables on team performance, considerable gaps in understanding these phenomena remain" (p. 581).

Diversity is about differences and can be defined in several ways to include the diversity of thought, ideas, color and gender. McVittie et al. (2008) pointed out, "Differences among employees create a more diversified workforce with a wide range of perspectives. Managing diversity means capturing the richness of these differences and harnessing them for the betterment of employees and the organization (Bartz et al. 1990, pp. 321-2)" (p. 349). The definition of diversity can vary based upon the group being questioned and at times can produce contentious or less than comfortable moments.

The diversity continuum encompasses a whole lot more than men vs. women, or white vs. black. Although different organizations understand diversity in the workplace differently, "diversity" as a concept has been gaining global attention. In the United Kingdom, for example, diversity quotas are being implemented in companies, while other European governments are imposing sanctions or withholding public service contracts from firms that do not comply with diversity rules (James 2009).

These new edicts have been embraced and celebrated in some places, and met with opposition and displeasure in others. Among various concerns, some believe that diversity requirements would result in unqualified minority candidates being hired only to fulfill a quota. Likewise, some organizations are concerned that they are now required to promote less qualified individuals into important roles they are not ready for. In response to these criticisms and concerns, James (2009) proposed that, "If equal opportunities are to be truly addressed; businesses and government should look at the reason why minorities are poorly represented within an organization, and seek to address that in a positive and constructive way" (p. 9).

The concern about minority candidates being less qualified is not unique to European soil. Some American companies, too, have questioned the diversity policies, and have seen their employees question the qualifications of the new manager, rather than accepting his credentials as they would with European American managers (Niehuis, 2005). However, it is no secret that organizations remain competitive when they support and implement continuous and transformational change (Gilley, Gilley, and McMillan, 2009). Some organizations will not change their ways or habits until they are forced to. For acceptance of changes to take place, Gilley et al. suggest there is a process, involving stages from awareness, interest, trial, to adoption.

Achieving Workplace Diversity

A key enabler to achieving workplace diversity is having a Board of Directors whose composition exemplifies diversity and represents the face of the consumers the company serves. Diversity in the boardroom can have direct impact on diversity in the workplace if diverse board members champion diversity within the organization. The championing of diversity is not an overt process, but can be embedded into expectations the board sets forth for leadership. The future of any firm requires talent management and succession planning, starting with securing talent within the organization to succeed the current leaders. If the boardroom does not display diversity, then the diversity expectations of the leadership team, or the construct of the employees, will be difficult to attain.

Singh (2007) cited two related theories that contribute to the lack of ethnic representation on boards: human capital theory and social capital theory. Reed, Srinivasan and Doty (2009) described human capital as a critical resource for differentiating financial performance among firms. Managing human capital requires attention both to knowledge stocks and knowledge flows. While it is important to maintain knowledge stocks by hiring competent individuals from the start, it is the intangible knowledge flows component of human capital-skill development and the ongoing institutionalization of firm and market-specific knowledge that firms must manage to maintain a fit with the competitive environment (p. 38).

Social capital theory, on the other hand, is an asset that resides in social relationships. Broadly speaking, according to Reed et al. (2009), social capitals reflect an organization's collective goal orientation and shared trust.

> These interactions may be formal ("typically documented with job descriptions and organizational charts") or informal ("people who know each other and help each other regardless of rank, function, or job title"). The greater the number of relationships and the higher the competence and credibility of the participants, the more value they provide. (p. 39)

In some cases, social capital would seem to trump human capital, because the phenomenon that "people who know each other and help each other regardless of rank, function or job title" has the potential to sway the hiring or appointing decision regardless of the person's skills. Granted, any successful organization would seek to appoint individuals to the Board who have the human capital or skills to perform the task. While resource dependency is focused on particular characteristics, which complement other board members, the addition of diversity can add value and benefit the overall organization.

Diversity, then, is a challenge for many organizations, as the representation of their board members are largely white men, as Fairfax (2005) observed,

> While women and people of color have
> experienced some increase in board
> representation over the last few decades,
> both groups also have encountered
> significant barriers to their success on
> corporate boards. However, people of color
> appear to have experienced more
> significant barriers than women, while
> women of color appear to be experiencing
> the most formidable of such barriers. (p.
> 1105)

Fairfax (2005) also mentioned, "Seventy-six percent of *Fortune* 1000 companies had at least one member of an ethnic minority on their board, comprised of 47% African Americans, 18% Latinos, and 11% Asian Americans" (p. 1107). The diverse boardroom composition sends a clear message to the organization on whether the company values diversity. Increasing the representation of African American men to senior management is the expected outcome of this study, prior to the appointments occurring there is a need to understand the dynamics African American men face in the workplace. The ensuing section on African American men in the workplace will provide that perspective.

African American Men and Black Rage in the Workplace

African American men face many obstacles in the workplace, being in the minority of employees, such as gaining access to opportunities, getting invited to after-work functions, and understanding the rules of engagement for survival in corporate America. Factors that contribute to these challenges – and the resultant frustration and "black rage" – especially in their pursuit of senior management positions include prejudice, discrimination, and the inability to function interpersonally in the white corporate environment (White, 2009). Many African American men feel they must conform to the white power structure or else they will not achieve any level of success. White (2009) describes the ills of conformity as a compromise, which causes ethnic minorities to compromise their identities, resulting in negative actions and behaviors in the workplace, such as anger, bitterness and depression.

Buttner, Lowe, and Billings-Harris (2006) believes the leaders' attitude toward diversity is one of the obstacles African American men experience in the workplace. If the leader has a high strategic goal regarding diversity, he is likely to be more engaged. But if the leader has a low strategic view of diversity, then he is less engaged. Buttner et al. also discovered when a leader has diversity measures on his performance review, his support of diversity initiatives is significantly higher.

Another area causing "black rage," the frustration of African Americans' upward struggle in the business world, is the perception of their employment as token hire. Some people, black or white, believe that African Americans are "token" hires, brought on the payroll simply as a statistic to meet a quota. This perception calls into question of whether African American employees add value to the organization (Martin, 2005). If the hiring of African American men is perceived as tokenism by other members of the organization, then the tenure of the individual will be wrought with grief trying to prove to them otherwise.

As indicated by White (2009), African American men become disenfranchised because of the lack of upward mobility within the organization, and this disenfranchisement reverts to anger. Many African American men have been labeled as angry or menacing because of stereotypes perpetrated in society (Hastings, 2008). The stereotype problem is two-fold and resides with white employers not being able to discern the difference of African American men as they layer their racial, biased, and stereotypical views across all African American men.

First, Zane (2002) found that "white men were convinced if they took a major diversity initiative, it would simply turn into another affirmative action program that undermined a system based on merit and obfuscated the problem of incompetent white female and black employees" (p. 342). When White men have stereotypical views of diversity programs it becomes practically impossible for African American men to succeed. The second part of the stereotypical thinking problem is African Americans are leery of certain jobs, such as sales, because of the stereotypes that upper level progression is not attainable. This thinking on the African Americans behalf refers to what Martin (2005) termed as the similarity attraction and social identity theory. In this theory people will only do business with people who act or look like them, so if African American men believes stereotypes are active in the workplace, there is a tendency for them to leave the environment, rather than face rejection.

White Privilege

On the other side of the coin is white privilege, which, according to McIntosh (as cited by Niehuis, 2005), is a "privilege whether in terms of race, gender, sexuality, or class is an invisible unearned asset that a person can count on cashing in each day" (p. 481). Boatwright and Soeung (2009) added that white privilege "refer to the many ways, typically invisible to White persons themselves, that white skin color is associated with prestige, privilege, and opportunities unavailable to other persons in society" (p. 574).

The presence of white privilege compounds the African American men's struggle upward into senior management positions. Many African Americans are raised in homes where their parents told them they must not only be as good as their white counterparts, but they must be better. For a majority of white men, however, being good was good enough.

Further establishing white privilege, Zane (2002) discovered, "Senior white males do not see the character of their White maleness and the ways they acted and reacted as White males to be a problem needing to be addressed" (p. 346). Although white men do not detect this racial nuance, African American men understand the situation. Kalev, Kelly, and Dobbin (2006) reported white men are becoming tired of having to constantly defend themselves in every discussion about diversity. Being the majority in the workforce and constantly having to hear about the changes they need to make, it is understandable why white men would feel the way they do. Both African American men and European American men are feeling frustration with the process of diversity and advancement, but working through the process is the only way progress will be made (Kalev, et al.). Understanding how African American men view the workplace can help leaders implement programs that begin to develop talent and feed the succession pipeline.

Successful implementation of talent management and succession plans begin with understanding how African American men perceive the process. Understanding why African American men appear to be angry, how white privilege impacts them, and how they are affected by stereotypes has a significant impact on successful talent-management and succession-planning plans.

Limiting Factor #4: Insufficient Talent Management

The fourth factor that limits African American men's journey into the executive suite and leading to the African American void is insufficient talent management. Talent management is the system of methods that organizations use to manage their talent, which is certainly impacted by the upper echelon theory, senior management decision making, and the accepted diversity practices of the organization. Though critical to the success and longevity of an organization, talent management is not always handled adequately, and can be fraught with anxiety and uncertainty. How talent is managed determines the path forward for African American men.

What *is* talent management?

While there may be no clear-cut definition, maintained Garrow and Hirsh (2008), they offered two perspectives of talent management: "Talent management is the systematic attraction, identification, development, engagement/retention, and the deployment of those individuals with high potential who are of particular value to the organization" (p. 390). Echoing the ambiguity of the term "talent management," Reilly (2008) noted, "Proposed definitions are, at worst, a mélange of different concepts strung together without a clear statement of what is meant by talent and how we might manage it" (p. 381).

In understanding talent management, Garrow and Hirsh (2008) focused on the concepts of "potential" and "particular value." The subjective determination of particular value can offset the significance of a person's potential. If certain groups of people are not perceived to be of particular value, then there is a good chance they will struggle to achieve, or will never achieve, value within the organization. The word potential can also be perceived as a curse because, rather than an asset, the word has a connotation of representing something that has yet to be achieved.

Adding to the difficulty of understanding talent management is that it can be mistaken as succession planning. The two terms are distinct and serve different purposes for organizational structure. Talent management is the process of developing the individual, while succession planning is the process of identifying individuals for certain roles. Once the individual is identified to succeed in a particular role, then their talent can be managed to evolve into the role they have been identified for. In addition, practically everyone can be considered talent within an organization and they can be managed appropriately, but not everyone in the organization will fit into a succession plan.

Talent management can evoke many questions. Garrow and Hirsch (2009) observed, "When mentioning the term talent management in many organizations, people get nervous. They start to wonder what do you mean by talent. Talent for what? Am I talent? What if I am not talent?" (p. 390). When these types of questions are asked in an organization, it typically belies the ineffective communication of its career development and talent management, irrespective of whether the employees are considered in a succession plan or not. In addition to feeding the succession pool, talent management also provides a means of developing or, if necessary, eliminating employees whose skills are not at the requisite level.

Talent Management Strategies

The aging workforce will force organizations to address their talent management programs. Nitasha (2007) predicted, "Over the next two decades 78 million baby boomers will turn 65 and the talent shortage will be significantly felt in the financial services, health care, engineering and education fields" (p. 44). This mass exodus of talent will place unprecedented pressure on organizations to fill the mind share of the departed employees, not to mention the headcount they represented. Knowing the workforce is going to be stressed for skilled labor, opportunities could abound for African American men to assume leadership positions in their respective industries and organizations.

Miller and Desmarais (2007) indicated three strategies organizations should be embraced to effectively compete for talent:

> (a) Talent development must begin with the identification of talented individuals, (b) development involves efforts to engage talent in organizational goals, and (c) talent development requires organizations to consider not only their present requirement for talent retention but also their future retention requirements. (p. 37)

In addition to the three strategies, Miller and Desmarais (2007) also indicated five best practices: "First, aligning leadership development with strategic initiatives, (b) getting the support of key stakeholders, (c) assessing the impact of culture, (d) linking leadership development to other HR processes, and (e) sustaining development through support of others" (pp. 38-41).

The intentions of best practices are to ensure an organization has the appropriate development of leaders within the organization. Though the concepts are broad reaching in scope of the participants, all five of the best practices can be beneficial in the furtherance of African American men in the workforce. The critical factor focuses on the management team's embracement of the concepts and the application of the best practices to this particular group of people. The third best practice of assessing the impact of culture is most relevant to the discussion of African American men in this study, yet the culture statement has little to do with color, but more to do with how business is conducted within the organization, i.e. how work is done, the times people arrive to work and with whom they collaborate.

Effective Talent Management Implementation

The effectiveness of a talent-management program hinges upon the receptiveness of the organization as a whole. How organizations embrace talent-management programs will determine how successful they can be and the process should extend beyond the human resource function. In many cases the responsibility for talent management is relegated to the human resource department, with little to no input from the management team. Cantrell and Benton (2007) specified, "Few organizations regularly undertake measurement and feedback–based improvement, executives surveyed reported that they seldom or never offered feedback and 78% of the organizations in their study had no tools or measurements to track and report workforce metrics" (p. 359).

Organizations should embrace the talent-management process beyond human resources and ensure employees are aware of the process. Though this study focuses on African American men, the process of managing talent is broader than the participants and talent management should not be afforded to a select group of individuals based upon nebulous criteria only known to senior leadership. Cantrell and Benton (2007) recommended, "To engage the hearts and minds of employees, an organization needs to establish trust and fair and consistent policies and processes‖ (p. 361). Cantrell and Benton discovered firms who practiced fair and consistent policies with talent management had employees who significantly impacted the firms' financial performance in a positive manner. Affecting the firms' financial performance should be the linchpin for every organization contemplating the implementation of a talent-management program. By demonstrating concern for the employee's development, the employee in return shows greater concern for the organizations success. The talent-management discussion is not a mystery in the sense of organization's experiencing success in developing their people, but there is an aspect of talent management that entreats exploration, which is the advent of coaching and how it is administered within the organization.

The development of talent elicits the implementation of an effective coaching process. McDermott, Levenson, and Newton (2007), quoted Conger stating, "Coaching is one of the great gold rushes in the field of leadership development" (p. 31). McDermott et al. (2007) discovered it matters a great deal regarding who provides the coaching as much as who receives the coaching. The person conducting the coaching must have an affinity for the process and the outcome of the individual. If there is not an inherent desire to see a person succeed, then the value of the coaching process is lost. Obviously the impact of an ineffective coach can lead to an ill-prepared candidate, but McDermott et al. (2007) also warned, "Ineffective coaching can lead to poor execution of business strategy and failed teamwork, reduced employee motivation and organization culture, along with poor communication and perceived management responsiveness" (p. 33).

Conversely, effective coaching can prove to be an effective tool enabling an organization to build their bench strength of talent and is summed up best by Steve Arneson, senior vice president of executive development at Capital One, (McDermott, et al. 2007)

> Coaching is critical part of our executive development strategy. We believe external coaches provide an independent stimulus for growth and development providing feedback and a clear plan to address developmental opportunities in a game changing way. With our coaching program, we're not merely trying boost performance and results; we're

looking for a deep bench of effective people
leaders for the company's future. (p. 32)

A company's approach to talent management will
determine the efficacy of the plan within the organization.
McDermott et al. cautioned, "Coaching was not a cure-all
for organizational issues, but the practice was certainly
effective in three key areas: (a) developing future leaders,
(b) improving leadership behaviors, and (c) improving
individual employee performances" (pp. 32-33).

Success can be attained when an organization embraces the
coaching process, and appropriately as well as
proportionally communicates the program within the
organization. Coaching is a key component of the overall
management of talent within an organization and the
succession-planning process can be enhanced by the
inclusion of the practice. The core of this study focuses on
the perceptions of succession planning with the African
American men and the practice of coaching can indicate
how well the succession-planning process is implemented.

Limiting Factor #5: Lack of Succession Planning

The fifth and last limiting factor in the African American
men's executive ascension is the lack of succession
planning in organization. Succession planning is
understood to be special efforts to invest in the best, highest
performing or highest potential talent at any organizational
level or function but particularly at or near the top (Barnett
& Davis, 2008). Hargreaves and Fink (2003) reviewed
succession planning from an educational background, and
indicated succession is connected to sustainability, which is

an organization's "ability to develop initiatives without compromising the development of others in the surrounding environment" (p. 694).

In order to have sustainable succession within an organization, three implications are apparent (a) proposing improvements applicable to everyone, (b) applying resources respectably and (c) not unnecessarily draining the organization's resources, and ensuring members of the team are effectively functioning in the new environment (Hargreaves & Fink, 2003).

As succession plans are introduced to the organization, there are knowledge phases successors will experience. Hargreaves (2005) identified three areas of knowledge within the transition of management and notes the components of inbound, inside, and outbound knowledge are implemented during the transition. Inbound knowledge is needed to make an impact on the organization, inside knowledge is gained as the leader becomes trusted and accepted in the organization, and outbound knowledge enables legacy's to continue along with the preservation of the organization.

Friedman (1986) described the succession process in a four-stage model to include (a) Establishing a need for the succession event, (b) determining selection criteria, (c) selecting candidates, and (d) choosing among the candidates‖ (p. 193). Since the early work of Friedman, much has been written and studied regarding succession planning, yet the tenets of succession planning remain the same, which is establishing a succession process and determining the best candidates. Succession planning systems are intended to help organizations manage their pipeline, and succession planning is defined as a structured process involving the identification and preparation of a potential successor to assume a new role (Barnett & Davis, 2008, p. 721). Barnett and Davis also indicated two outcomes of implementing succession plans: First, the process helps to identify the level of leadership talent the organization has, and second, succession planning can enable the organization to continue to learn and grow the most talented individuals in the organization. In addition, Fegley (as cited in Barnett & Davis, 2008) discussed a recent study on succession planning and reported, "Fifty-eight percent of the respondents communicated their organization had some level of succession planning, 26% of the respondents communicated they intended to develop one, and 16% stated they had no intention of developing a succession planning system‖ (p. 722).

With the potential of 42% of organizations not having a succession-planning system or process, the challenge for African American men begins with the organization developing a succession-planning process. Richard, Wright, Ferris, Hiller, and Kroll (as cited in Greer & Virick, 2008) determined, "An emerging body of empirical evidence indicates positive performance effects for diversity, and there are increasing indicators of the strategic importance of diversity to the success of companies" (p. 352). The next challenge is ensuring the succession-planning process is communicated or is inclusive of African American men. As indicated by the data, many organizations have done little to react to the overall problem of succession planning and fewer have developed plans to address succession planning for African American men.

Succession Planning Strategies

McNamara, Watson, and Wittmeyer, (2009) outlined a four-step process of CEO succession planning (Passmore and Torres, 2007) with the first phase consisting of assessing the situation to include timing and the candidate pool, the second phase consists of engagement of the CEO and the board regarding conducting a search, the third phase consists of the actual search and selection, with the CEO deciding to pursue an internal or external candidate, and the final step involves the transfer of power.

Compiling the work of McNamara et al. and Friedman, the most critical common step to the succession process is the selection of candidates. The selection process will determine how effective the transition of the individual and company will be. Hargreaves (2005) identified planned continuity and discontinuity as outcomes of the succession process. Much of the continuity hinges upon the selection process and planned continuity is attained when plans are well thought out and build upon the goals and accomplishments of the predecessor.

As indicated in Phase 3 (McNamara et al. 2009), two resources for applicants are considered—internal and external candidates. The preference is typically an internal candidate because the downtime of the position is limited due to the new leader already having a grasp of the structure and processes of the organization. The cost associated with promoting internal candidates is typically less as well since relocation may not be involved in the appointment depending upon where the applicant resides. The internal choice is also viewed favorably because the messages delivered to the organization are employees are rewarded for loyalty and hard work. The external candidate also provides value to the organization. Bringing in outside talent enables the organization to provide a heterogeneous approach to process and management style. In some organizations change may be needed to enable the organization to recognize threats and pursue opportunities with a different vigor. However, the external candidate does come with some risk, as Vollhardt (2005) indicated,

> While hiring externally to fill a newly vacated senior role is perhaps the riskiest scenario, an internal successor also faces considerable challenges and an unacceptably high risk of a difficult transition. According to research by Manchester Inc., four out of ten newly promoted managers and executives fail, i.e., are terminated, perform below expectations, or voluntarily resign within 18 months of starting their new jobs. The reasons cited for failure include lack of performance, inability to set clear expectations with their boss, failure to successfully integrate with the corporate culture, inability to engage in teamwork with staff and peers, and lack of internal business savvy. (pp. 3-4)

Altman (2009) identified —During uncertain times it is more important than ever to know where key talent sits within an organization and how to develop people to meet short and long-term business critical issues‖ (p. 74). Altman also recommended line managers should own the succession process with direct alignment from the chief executive officer as well as HR. The three-layered approach provides the proper level of ownership from key constituents within the organization.

Effective Succession Planning Implementation

To accomplish successful succession planning an organization benefits from having a holistic view of talent within the organization. The reality is many organizations still do not have effective succession plans in place. Thompsen (2009) revealed, ―Despite having anticipated C-Suite vacancies within the year, about half of organizations lack a succession plan for C-Suite executives, reflecting an overwhelming lack of preparedness to fill those vacancies‖ (p. 15). Thompsen identified a major gap of succession planning typically focuses on the CEO, when the plans should start with junior executives.

Thompsen (2009) also offered five strategies for organizations to prepare themselves for successful transitions of leadership to include (a) sifting the noise, (b) creating a line of sight (c) aligning performance, (d) exploring ideas, and (e) lobbying. Sifting the noise involves managers understanding the critical nature of the communication and knowing what is not being said. Creating a line of sight involves senior management building focus at every level and commitment to the plan of record. Aligning performance mandates senior management recognize performance that contributes to the advancement of goals and correct performance when off-track. Exploring ideas involves leaders proactively seeking new ways of conducting business and facilitating cross-functional knowledge. Lobbying involves working collaboratively by gaining consensus through communication and securing resources needed to accomplish the goal.

Considering Thompsen's five strategies, it is worthy to note none of these strategies are gender specific, race specific, or education specific. The non-specificity of gender, race, and education is significant because if gender, race, and education are not significant in the strategy, then a logical thought is the faces of those who are hired or promoted to the top positions in an organization should not have the same face. Yet, in a large percentage of organizations, White men still hold the majority of top positions.

In order for succession plans to be effective for an employee in general, Berchelman (2005) articulated, Inaccurate assessments of where talent is lacking can blindside a company. We need to know which spots will be empty in coming years and what new spots will be created as the company grows. Only then will early identification of key talent allow companies to proactively develop leaders for the future. In short, the solution is to identify, assess, and develop. (p. 12)

In the case of African American men, inaccurate assessments may have been made regarding their abilities to perform junior executive roles, which lead to senior executive roles. This inaccurate assessment is potentially aligned to the perceptions of the study participant's and core to the problem of African American men's ascension to the executive suite.

The current business environment has organizations downsizing their workforce, and businesses declaring bankruptcy, it is extremely important organizations ensure they have a process for succession plans. The plans within the organization cannot focus on a few leaders, rather to properly prepare for the future; the organization should take a holistic view of the organizations' needs. Rudis (2006) interviewed Dow Corning Corporation chair, president, and CEO, Stephanie A. Burns, and added where I think we're falling down, and I would guess that other companies are similar, in Europe and the United States is around diversity. We can attract and retain top talent, but we aren't always getting the diverse mix that we're seeking—namely, passport diversity, gender diversity, and ethnic background diversity. My second concern is that, in Asia, we're struggling to find the top talent, and when we do, we struggle to retain it. I actually think we retain talent better than benchmarks. But you invest, you train, you acculturate, and, very often, you lose people. (pp. 52-53)

An additional area of focus is the decision to procure talent from within or outside of the organization. The decision to hire from within sends the message the organization is committed to developing talent within the organization. Attracting talent outside of the organization can send a signal to internal candidates of their diminished worth to the organization. When making the decision to succeed with an internal candidate or external candidate, Altman (2009) cautioned organizations to look within for replacements and understand the qualities and qualifications needed for future managing directors or chief executive roles. Promoting from within has benefits as the employee is immediately competent regarding the knowledge of the industry and company products. However, hiring from the outside may afford the organization a different pair of lens on the construct of the organization, which potentially adds value to the organizations' business model.

Throughout the research on succession planning the commentary continued to focus on the individual and his background of skills. Very seldom has a CEO mentioned diversity or the desire to present a different face to Wall Street or the community at large. However, the core of this study seeks to understand the perceptions of the African American men experiences with succession planning and if the senior levels of the organization continue to say they are focused on the most qualified candidate, yet they have not widened their search of candidates beyond those who look like them or are in leadership positions close to them, the cycle may never be broken.

Cingoranelli (2009) offered another view on succession planning with several tips to ensure an organization is prepared for the future to include (a) create an environment that facilitates succession transition, (b) nurture future leaders, (c) align elements of key partner retirement agreements, and (d) evaluate the elements of a successful compensation system (pp. 44-46). All four tips are applicable to succession planning, but the article does not address diversity with the exception of focusing on younger leaders, because the cycle to train the next CEO could run up to five years. The article made no mention of gender or color as decision criteria for succession planning.

Lastly, Dutton (2009) offered several steps to effectively implement a succession planning process within an organization to include,

(a) Meet with the CEO to clarify expectations of any succession plan, (b) get leaders in the room and walk them through the process of revising the succession plan. Ask if it supports the company's vision, strategy, and values, (c) identify future talent needs, (d) establish competencies for key positions, (e) help employees plan their careers and bridge their own skill gaps, (f) look internally and externally for expertise and (g) assign promising employees to talented and compatible mentors. (p. 45)

Dutton (2009) identified steps to effectively implement a succession-planning process, but does not mention the need to diversify the group. If the decisions are unchecked then the group will choose participants who mirror themselves. The process of succession planning becomes lucid, but the process of selecting candidates is ambiguous.

The succession-planning process is the culmination of the five steps identified in the conceptual diagram. The conceptual diagram begins with the upper echelon theory that espouses organizational outcomes are predicted by managerial background and characteristics (Hambrick and Mason, 1984). The composition of the senior management team is directly derived from the beliefs, thoughts and practices from other mangers. If senior management champions diverse practices then when talent-management discussions happen, outcomes are more diverse. If the senior management team does not advocate diversity then the homogenous management team is in full effect. The last step in the conceptual diagram is the actual succession plan and the administration of the candidates. Succession planning represents the cycle where the inclusion of African American men within senior management structures begins or ends.

PART II

AFRICAN AMERICAN MEN IN EXECUTIVE SUITES: HOW TO FILL THE VOID

CHAPTER 3

Stories of Successful African American Men's Journey into the Executive Suite

At the outset of this project, I was interested in understanding the factors that limit or promote African American men's executive ascension. Having gained an overview of the limiting factors in Part I of this book, I now take you to factors that promote executive ascension. To understand what "works" and what doesn't in climbing the corporate ladder, I set out to find success stories of those who have made it, so to speak. This phenomenological study focused on the lived experiences of African American men and their perceptions of talent management and succession planning at the senior management level within American corporations. The ten corporate executives I interviewed very graciously and willingly shared their lived experiences with succession-planning and talent-management programs. Their hope – and mine – is that by retelling their stories, the next generation of capable African American men will be better equipped to succeed in obtaining senior management positions.

Interview Structure

For each interview, I followed an Interview Guide (see Figure 2 on next page) designed to home in on these ten executives' experiences in succession planning and talent management.

APPENDIX B. Interview Guide

#1 Talent Management

1. Is training or employee development offered in your organization?
2. How do employees in your organization get promoted?
3. How would you describe your career path approach?
    a. What strategies have you employed to get promoted?
    b. What would you do differently?
    c. What type of training programs have you experienced?
4. How many times have you been promoted?
    a. What were the job(s) you were promoted from/to?
    b. How did the promotion(s) occur?
    c. Did you have to relocate for any of the position(s)?
    d. Describe the nature of the job or promotion you received.

#2 Succession Planning

1. Does your company have a succession planning process?
2. Do you have formalized mentoring in your organization?
3. Are senior management level opportunities communicated within the organization?
4. Does your manager conduct performance reviews with you?
    a. What are the frequencies of the reviews?

Figure 2. Interview Guide.

Each interviewee was an African American man who had ascended to the minimum level of director in his organization, and each had tenure of more than 18 years within their respective organizations or industry. Their ages were 40 years old and above. All interviewees were actively involved or engaged in the succession-planning and talent-management process within their respective company. The location of the interviewees spanned from the Midwest (4), to the South (4) and to the Northeast (2), with none from the Western states. The 10 interviewees are given pseudonyms in this book as summarized in Table 2.

Table 2. Participant Demographics

Code	Tenure	Age	Title	Education	Times Promoted	Location
"Ralph"	15+	40+	Director	Undergraduate	5+	MW
"James"	25+	50+	Vice President	Undergraduate	15+	NE
"Henry"	20+	40+	Director	Graduate	5+	S
"Alfred"	15+	40+	Director	Graduate	5+	MW
"Scott"	30+	50+	Vice President	Undergraduate	5+	MW
"Edward"	30+	50+	Director	Graduate	< 5	NE
"Jason"	30+	50+	Director	Undergraduate	5+	S
"Gary"	15+	50+	Director	Undergraduate	5+	S
"Robert"	30+	50+	Director	Undergraduate	15+	MW
"Marquis"	20+	40+	President	Undergraduate	< 5	S

The education level of interviewees ranged from an associate degree to MBA, with 30% of the members having an MBA, 60% having a bachelor's degree, and 10% having an associate degree. All participants relocated more than once for a promotional career opportunity and the minimum number of times each participant was promoted was 4 times with the maximum number of promotions being 20.

In this chapter, I will allow the summarized experiences of the executives to give you a flavor of their upward journey into the executive suite. These words were given in their response to the question "How do you describe your experience with reaching senior management positions within your company?"

In Chapter 4, I will outline for you the major themes that emerged from their responses, which can serve as 7 tips for success in your own journey.

How do you describe your experience with reaching senior management positions within your company?

"**Ralph**" did not view his experience as unique and he perceived what happened to him happens to a lot of people.

> With Acme Technology I would probably have become a VP at this point, at least three years ago, but certain things happened, we transformed the HR organization, I took another role in a division that was sold off as part of the divestiture. At that point I made a decision to leave the organization because my role decreased in scope, and if everything stayed the same…which is a naïve comment…if everything stayed the same structure wise I felt confident that the achievements that I was gaining… the success I was having would've led me to that senior level. I think it's going to take probably a move to a smaller organization to get to that VP level role. Having now

switched employers three times in the last five years, so it's one of those situations where I am encouraged and motivated because I believe that I built a very strong background of experience to get to the next level, but it's very difficult to get to transfer to a new organization at the VP level without having been a VP before. That's my challenge but it's something that I am prepared for.

"James" viewed his career path was mostly prescriptive, meaning there were roles and responsibilities that needed to be accomplished before he could go to the next role.

I skipped a level which required having to move to the corporate office and felt I had a couple of different tracks that others did not have. I also felt the approach was traditional and my journey was not necessarily unique, it was not totally different from my Caucasian counterparts. I really feel that someone had a vested interest in me and they said I should have that job and if that does not happen for an individual then the person is not going to get the job…it just doesn't happen like that…that's why people leave the organization…you have to have a voice behind you in succession planning meetings to be successful.

"Henry" discussed his journey as having to play the game and identified areas where he may have held his own career progression back because of the choices he made, yet he was comfortable with the outcome.

You have to have major sponsorship and be willing to play the game. Almost to the point to where it seems to me that that's really all you kinda do, it feels to me like you rise on not on what you know, but who you know. That's terrible to say that but that's just my jaded view. The game entails… How can I put this…thinking about it from my perspective where I am right now in terms of if I wanted to really go after positional power and become somebody's vice president, as far as what that would really entail I would have to go sacrifice my own personal set of comfort things to come up here and be president with you guys, I'm going to work out of some northeast city, I am going to pull 16 hour days just for the sake…so in other words it feels to me like there are certain situations where activity is misconstrued as achievement as opposed to the other way around. It's basically it's like I want to come and make you feel very comfortable with me and you begin to like me so that you will consider me for this particular kind of job as opposed to basing it on the merits of my accomplishments and capabilities. Saying you know what, this guy is pretty good at this so let's give him this job. I may not be comfortable with him but it's like I am very comfortable with how he thinks and what he does, so in other words it feels like the very essence of the way we claim diversity, it's hypocritical at best. Because we will identify and we will say it's central and tantamount to…it's the linchpin of the success of our organization but we don't embrace it because at the end of the day, if we did then you look at senior management and it would be a diverse slate of candidates or a diverse slate of folks, but it's just not. The fact that we value diversity is contradictory because they say it and it's baked into the leadership model but when you look at the senior levels of the organization they don't look like the words that these guys are saying, so in other words do as I say not as I do. To me it's like when you really want to get down to it, put your money where your mouth is and go out…there are an abundance of highly qualified African Americans, Hispanics, Asian Americans, Indians, whatever that they could…. Diversity to me doesn't mean that it's gotta be all Black folks! (animated) not at all, not at all…we play in a global economy. At this point and so to me it's like…and the fall back on that too is they'll say well it's not necessarily the outcome of how you look, but it's diversity of thought… So how does that work when you have a bunch of White folks with shared experiences, who think alike, so to me it's like when you say you value something you have a Chief Diversity Officer…I met this woman who worked for "Western Energy" and she seems like a really good person, but at the end of the day, I'm like okay, this isn't a sitcom, she sees what's happening for real, there's no piped in laughter, the senior levels of the organization did not look like what she's been brought here to drive and actually affect that change, so I'm like what are you doing, how can you really believe that, and how do they expect other folks to believe it…. don't talk about it, be about it, show me, that's my perspective!

"Alfred" discussed the mirror image concept, where people are making decisions on hiring based upon those that resemble them.

For me the process is doable, but the issue is timing and the organization wanting to have a diverse organization. I have been told that I am capable and I'm on track, I have found that networking is key, so when a job does open up and people are talking about me in the succession-planning process. Inherently I have found that people are hiring people who look like them and act like them. Having a pipeline is critical.

"Scott" spoke about an internal drive that propelled him to success.

> I think the experience was rewarding that required a lot of work and a lot of trials and tribulations because it wasn't as if I was born with that…It required work, required networking, it required communication, required improvement of my education skills as well as my communication skills but when I look back at it, it was rewarding in terms of achievement. I look at what I wanted to accomplish after leaving college and to achieve the best I could do at the highest level that I could achieve. So there was a drive that would say hey you know this is what I need to do a little bit more of, I need to get into this position, and I had to do that, so I had the drive to do it and as look back at it I feel satisfied that I did have that drive and most of it was as I said self-promotion in the beginning, but with that it still made such that it got me to where I needed to be.

"Edward" was one of the first to introduce the theme of intentionality. He discussed doing things with intention, not solely for personal gain, but really having a purpose and direction about the activities he was involved in.

> My journey has been to remain open to possibilities, opportunities, networking is invaluable, I did it early in my career sort of

haphazardly, the latter part of my career I came to understand the necessity for being intentional around building relationships and having the focus and understanding that it's a give-and-take kind of dynamic, that I have a responsibility to nurture relationships…workwise as well as socially. That's been the biggest aha for me when I think back to then and now, I read once that people who have an unconditional self-regard for themselves and others are considered to be socially graceful, but those individuals that can build relationships and sustain them and demonstrate them as a mutual benefit to oneself as well as the other person in the relationship, if you can do that and really be clear about what the benefits are, you're considered to be socially skillful, and that was my biggest lesson learned…. how to be more socially skillful, I always felt that relationships required you to like people and to be liked and I just missed the boat when I look back so many times, it's not about being liked or liking, it's about personal development and the mutual benefit that two people can derive from a relationship.

"**Jason**" along with several other participants identified being the first person of color in their organization to get a promotion, achieve a task, or be a part of a program. "Jason" provides perspective on why being a trailblazer was difficult and how he managed to become successful when the odds were against him.

> I believe this was a very difficult journey because I was the first senior director of human resources that was a person of color in the organization that I am aware, and clearly I thought I should've been a VP long ago. The senior director position was positioned just directly below the VP and in many organizations the position I held would've easily been a VP position without a doubt, because of the reporting responsibility and the type responsibility that I had. Looking over the scope of things way back when, it was not as important to be a VP as it was to make the money and have the authority and the power within the organization so I formed a game plan and my plan was to be connected, to have as much authority and power as I could in the organization, and get compensated for it. During my career I was compensated on par with most of the VPs if not more. There are many times I was making more than the VP and was getting more stock options than VPs, and more bonus than the VPs, because they valued what I was contributing to the company. I made a point of taking on the toughest assignments and doing some things that were very high risk.

As an example in one plant they're trying to organize a union I was the lead person from human resources to lead the defense against the union organizing activity, at the same time in another plant that was in the process of trying to decertify I headed up both of those from an HR standpoint. They were going on simultaneously I was successful in both cases to certify one plant and fight off the union organization in the other plant and for those efforts I was awarded the highest award in the company. When we had another problem the CEO of the company and the president of the region asked me to fight off another decertification attempt and I did and I was awarded the President's award because we had 22 negotiation sessions and we never got to the point of talking finances and the Teamsters walked away from that organization and we ended up decertifying the union. Plus with many plant closings I was the head of those closings and they're all done without any violence, all of them were handled flawlessly from an HR perspective and the business perspective. I took most of the cases and I would have the VP and senior VPs call me before me I left home in the morning to talk about stuff that we were going to do during the day. I made my point it was not the title, it was really, it was important, it was really having the power and decision-making skills that they would value that would get you ahead.

I could've left the organization several times for vice president positions that were offered to me, but when I did the analysis on those positions I would not have the authority and the power and the ability to play in the mix of making major decisions that I had in the job that I had.

"Gary" described the mystery this study sought to discover that is how effective are succession plans for African American men within organizations.

I would say the experience has been null and void. I had not had a conversation with anyone that articulates what it takes to get on the radar for a senior management position. Was I even in the running? Was I qualified? It really is getting the cart before the horse, the horse is when the individual calls, can you actually do the job and I know that when the next job is open I should have a chance. The cart is when the position is open it is filled before anyone even knows about it. Very few people even know a job is going to be open and had I known the job was open then I could have tried to throw my name in for the job. A lot of the issue is not knowing the job is open and what the criteria was. They give you the customary you are doing a good job, but when the job opens they do not call. I hope that this study will help other Brothers and Sisters.

"Robert" took a holistic approach and discussed the highs and lows of his journey along with providing perspective on how to take responsibility for yourself and not rely on others to make things happen for you.

It has been a very good experience for me, I got to some very high positions, I was compensated very highly, I was able to retire at a young age, and I have all my hair (chuckles) and I knew when it was time to leave. For me...... it's not that way for everyone along the way some people leave and I learned early on sometimes you have to have a little bit more patience on certain things. At certain times in your career things change, you know you're not thought of as the golden boy anymore or the golden person. You have to figure out can you adjust to that, are you comfortable within that or do you need to pick up... I always thought that you are free agent, and if you kept that in mind you manage your career, you manage yourself, and don't let no one take control of you. A lot of times we get caught up, and I think particularly in this economy right now there is little fear out there that people are kind of afraid to exercise those rights that they have, and the right is that you have the right to be a free agent and go somewhere else if this doesn't work for me here. Over time you're going to run across a person that's an asshole in your career and you've got to deal with them, and you gotta look yourself in the mirror, even though I was set up on this or if I don't think I was wrong you have to put the onus on yourself and take responsibility for yourself. When you take responsibility for yourself; I guarantee you the success in terms of how you feel about yourself and never let someone take control of your destiny. That's the way I woke up every morning that way, it wasn't an arrogant…… it was just… I'm going to take responsibility for myself and if something happens or if it didn't happen in the right way, then it's my fault.

"Marquis" clearly placed the onus of his career progression on himself. He didn't accept "no" as an answer and constantly strived for improvement. His journey ultimately led him out of the corporate environment and into a sole proprietorship.

Overall I would say it was positive I've never once been in a position where I felt that it was unattainable, I've never been in a position where I felt someone was excluding me or not giving me the information for me to accomplish it. Yes I think it was very positive, I didn't get there [senior management] because I left, I moved on, I wanted to start my own practice. When I left the last practice I was with after I went in and talked with senior partner, one of the partners came over and sat down with me and had a very conscientious conversation and he asked me why I was leaving and I said from the time I graduated from college I had this itch to become…start my own practice and before I become a partner in a firm I have to know…I have to know whether or not I could do it another way. Because once you become a partner in another firm, big firms like that one, that's a lifer position. You don't walk away from a position like that, the firm is 50+ years old, and you don't walk away from that position, not easily. So I said, I gotta know, there are aspects of the management side that I was frustrated with from the standpoint of not knowing. One of the partners came to me and said we respect you a great deal and I believe that because I was vocal about some things when it came to what we were being asked to do as project managers. We were being asked to keep the projects profitable and one of the things they had done is they held a management course and this course lasted for several weeks, actually several months, and every Wednesday we would get all the project managers together and talk about something specific. One of the meetings we were going over project sheets, these are financial sheets, and I interrupted the meeting and I said these numbers don't work, and the senior partner was in there and the senior-level finance person and he said what do you mean, and I showed them this number and that number and that number and they don't work, and the finance person got a little defensive and said sure they do, I've [Marquis] been studying them [the numbers] for almost 6 months now... because you put us in a position where we have to make profit, we have to respond to these management sheets, the numbers don't work, I keep sending them back to you, telling you to change a certain number, and it never gets changed. He looked at it and right at that point... what I said and it had been that way, and each one of them started looking at their sheets and I was the only one or one of the few people in that management group that would say, you know what I want to do exactly what I've been asked to do and more. So I began to study those numbers and it was true something was off in the number system and after that day I never saw the sheet again. I was invested, I was invested personally and professionally, I believe in every practice that I've been in I've been emotionally, professionally invested in what's going on and I believe that that is important for you or any individual, especially African-Americans. It's important for us to be invested in order for anybody to promote us, in order for anybody to feel like you're the guy, it's unfortunate for me to say that but I do believe that. I believe that we or there is an impression out there about us... doesn't exactly put us in that light as soon as somebody sees us coming.

General Perceptions on the Effectiveness of Talent Management and Succession Planning

The interviewees shared their collective experiences and demonstrated the process of being included in talent-management programs required them to perform and then gain recognition from management of their abilities. In some cases they had to push or fight for the recognition of their performance. The perceptions of the participants' organizations talent-management processes call into question the gap in the upper echelon theory perceptual process that potentially allows management to neglect their responsibilities; the onus is placed on the employee to not just perform at a high level but also engage in self-promotion.

The potential gap in the upper echelon theory perceptual process will be discussed in greater detail in Chapter 5. In general the interviewees understood how the talent-management process worked and they were informed of what they could do to enhance their careers. However, some believed the mystery still existed regarding how people are placed in certain roles.

While Fegley (as cited in Barnett and Davis, 2008) indicated 58% of organizations have a succession-planning process, 40% of the executives I interviewed reported that their organizations had a succession-planning process. For effective succession-planning, 7 themes were derived from the interviewees' responses and outlined in the next chapter, which can provide a roadmap for African American men who aspire to attain senior-level management positions in a corporation.

CHAPTER 4

Roadmap to the Executive Suite: 7 Practical Steps to Success

The journey to the executive suite in corporate America will vary from individual to individual, but as you have already seen in the last chapter, the ten executives who shared their stories have experienced many similar struggles in their own journeys. As I analyzed their interview responses, using the Atlas.ti software, which allowed for the triangulation of responses into singular themes, seven themes emerged regarding their patterns of behavior and/or thought processes.

Forming the acrostic "PINDOWN," the seven tips have served those ten executives well, and can help you pin down the secret to success in your executive ascension journey:

Proactive

Intentional

Network

Driven by Performance

Ownership

White Female Colleagues' Impact

Never Give Up

The executives I interviewed expressed a genuine desire to give back to their communities and give pointers to those who followed their trails. By sharing their success stories, they hope they will help the next generation of African American men avoid the same difficulties, or at least have the resources to deal with certain situations. Their desire is aptly captured in a comment made by "Gary" at the end of his interview, and echoed by all other executives: "I hope that this…will help other Brothers and Sisters."

Step 1: Be Proactive

Being proactive is a critical component to career growth, and this attitude was crucial in the interviewees' success in dealing with exclusion from promotions, training program participation, career path approach and the performance review process. Thornberry and White (2008) understand "being proactive" to mean "taking conscious control over your life, setting goals and working to achieve them" (p. 26). Many of the interviewees commented on how they took control of their careers to get to the point where they were, while others recalled the times they were not proactive enough and how it hindered their careers.

Being Proactive in Training Programs

"Ralph" realized he had an experience gap in working with unions and realized if he was going to be successful, he would have to gain the knowledge of working with unions to be more effective in his job. He said, "Working with unions very early in my career, I think it allowed me to be more proactive with employee relations strategies to head things off at the pass before they became issues."

"Marquis" stressed the importance of being proactive in regards to participating in training programs, stating,

> In our profession there is a tri-headed coordination, architect and engineers, contractors and owners..... with contractors the big shtick is architects just live in their office and they don't know anything about construction, they don't know how to put things together, they just know how to draw, by getting the construction aspect and becoming a Carpentry Mason Specialists it gave me a leg up on everybody else. I actually went out and built helicopter pads, I constructed barracks, we constructed demolition bunk heads, so I had to learn a portion of the business that was totally outside of what we normally do and I believe that that assisted me, that helped me and showed me an aspect that was not necessarily provided to me, but was a part of my own doing, unknowingly assisted me.

Being Proactive in Performance Reviews

"James" demonstrated his proactivity in his preparation for the performance discussion, reminding us that "You don't want issues to arise in the 11th hour about a situation that needs to be resolved and be more proactive than reactive."

"Gary" also shared his experience of getting a promotion with a proactive attitude:

You have to be up front and demanding as
to what it takes to get promoted and
document with follow ups–90 days or 1
year. Unless you put it in writing for the
criteria for promotion then it probably
won't happen. I also had communication
with the manager's manager to ensure there
was alignment. My process demonstrated
that I was holding my manager accountable
and my manager's manager noted as well.
The outcome would allow for conversation
to happen to explain why I didn't get a
promotion in case I was passed over.

Being Proactive in Career Management

"Henry" spoke on the price of being proactive in terms of
career management,

Thinking about it from my perspective
where I am right now in terms of, if I
wanted to really go after positional power
and become somebody's vice president, as
far as what that would really entail I would
have to go sacrifice my own personal set of
comfort things to come up here and be
president with you guys, I'm going to work
out of some northeast city and I am going to
pull 16 hour days just for the sake. So in
other words it feels to me like there are
certain situations where activity is
misconstrued as achievement as opposed to
the other way around.

"Alfred" echoed this point, sharing that

> Early in my career I would do more to
> understand the requirements of a job and not
> go blindly into the role. Later in my career I
> would focus on a higher level of
> understanding of strategy, where the
> organization is trying to go.

Being Proactive When Excluded from Promotion

When discussing how he handled the exclusion from promotion, "Scott" advocated proactive strategies,

> I would take an accounting course if I felt
> that I was not really sharp in the area of
> budgets and those types of things. So I take
> an accounting course external to the
> organization and utilize that and let it be
> known that I took this course to strengthen
> myself in this area soon…..when the
> position became available they couldn't use
> well, —you're not strong in this particular
> area…….. If it was something that the
> organization did not fund but if I felt it was a
> need, then I would take a course in local
> community colleges that were available in
> the area.

"Robert" also brings up the importance of a proactive attitude, which could result in promotions.

> Even though that job was out of my comfort
> zone, I found that I had to go on my own

and get some training and meet people outside of the company that could provide me with skills where I could be successful. Obviously I was successful in that job when after 14 months a coworker left the company and I was promoted to his position which was a two-level promotion.

"Jason" also experienced the cost of a less-than-proactive attitude for a business professional:

I was formally told I was not getting the job by the senior vice president who was in charge of the function. I had a conversation with the senior vice president to find out why I was not the successful candidate for that position. The explanation that he gave me was not acceptable because he I said wasn't ready for that job and that the candidate was better and I told him I disagreed with that and told him the next time the job came up I wanted it and I asked him what did I need to do to make sure I was a lead candidate when the job came back up.

Being Proactive in Career Approach

"Edward" described how he was proactive in his career approach:

For a long time I truly just did what I thought was the best thing based upon my interests, based upon what I wanted to do, jobs I wanted to have. I thought in terms of jobs versus career, it wasn't until I left graduate school that I began to think more in terms of career and began to look at activities that I engaged in and how do they fit, do they really provide steppingstones to future opportunities for me.

Step 2: Be Intentional

Intentionality is another central element in the ten executives' responses regarding talent-management and succession-planning, although this has not been a concept identified in existing literature as a key mechanism for progressing in the organization. Each of the ten executives made conscious choices to separate themselves from the pack; they were intentional in their actions to get to the next level. Brass and Haggard (2010) argued that "intentional action not only involves a decision when to act and what action to execute, but also the decision whether to act or not" (p. 604).

Some of the intentional actions taken by the interviewees included self-improvement and some involved enlisting the help of others. Regardless of the specific actions taken, the executives were focused on doing something different.

Being Intentional about Self-Improvement and Seeking Mentorship

"Ralph" shared about how he developed his skills within his organization:

I addressed this by starting to get out of my own box, I invited people out to lunch that I would normally wouldn't, I started to stop by people's office and just started talking about their jobs and comparing notes to what I was doing and how that was benefiting the business.

Being Intentional about Obtaining Promotion

"James" stressed the importance of advocating on your own behalf intentionally:

I tried to be recognized at being excellent at what I did. Unless that happens you won't be recognized. Not understanding the organization has programs for fast trackers and not knowing caused people to be at a disadvantage. I tried to make sure that the role at hand was recognized…as easily recognized as by the decision makers. I tried to be an excellent people manager and the organization saw that I could prepare folks to move forward and that made me standout from the others.

"Henry" shared a similar experience:

In 2004 I received a major award which should've been my third award, but if you don't have a sponsor then it's very difficult to get the visibility that you need, but it seemed like all the planets aligned correctly back in 2004. I worked very close with my managers and made them look good, and I felt like I was in a really sweet spot so I really turned it on and opened up all eight cylinders, not only did I work harder but also smarter. I kept people in the loop in making sure that everybody was tuned in. All the while not hinting that I'm going to get my reward now, but I had my eye on the spot and I would like it to come to this or I would like to move to that, or just out and out ask them.

"Scott" spoke further on self-promoting:

I felt you had to self-promote because at that time if you didn't promote yourself it was not hard for the organization to just look over your background and say, What about this person? What about that person? It was something at the timeline that if you are interested in something, then you basically had to let someone know that you're interested in it or you are always just overlooked or bypassed. Whether that was by design or just lack the resources in the HR area, I just felt that if it was something that I wanted I had to be my own promoter.

"Robert" also shared about intentional strategies he used to secure promotion:

I surrounded myself around people that were performing at high levels and a lot of times these were people that were senior to me. I asked them what did it take for them to become successful and what did it take for them to get to that position. I understood the organization inside and out. I understood the position as you take it on and assignments that you take on that would help you accelerate your promotion.

On the other hand, "Jason" focused his attention on networking as a strategy to be promoted:

I also focused on networking with people that were in decision-making positions that would have some input into whether or not if I were able to receive a promotion. I established my network by learning the culture of the organization I was in and I made sure that I interfaced with the people that were influential in the whole advancement planning or promotion process, starting with my immediate supervisor.

"Marquis" also recalled one particular encounter that showed him the importance of being intentional in order to be promoted in the organization:

When I got into the firm there was a guy who had been there for quite a while and he and I had a private conversation and he asked me or I asked him, "You been here for a while why aren't you partner? And he didn't know why, that was a sign to me that I am going to know why. I'm going to know why. So the one time that I asked the company what are the steps to become partner and this was after the time that I became senior associate and I knew that was the next step. I said tell me how, and they said we actually have a list and they gave me the list.... well these are the things that we want to see out of you in order to… before we even consider it…. 75% of the lists I had, they were all done. I was actually doing 85% of the things in the list. The last couple of pieces and parts, you need to bring in some clients, even though your job is not to do that, you bring in some clients that's the next step and that was probably one of the primary reasons or things you had to accomplish in order to become partner.

Being Intentional about Career Approach

"Alfred" said on the point about being intentional in your career approach, "I looked at the next job and comprehended what the core competency and measured up where I was against those requirements versus where my current skills are and I developed an action plan to improve my skills."

Step 3: Network – Find a Mentor

All of the executives were quick to acknowledge that "no one gets here on his own." Having a mentor was a critical component in rising to the next level. Mentors are people who are able to help maneuver careers through organizations. Taylor, Taylor, and Stroller (2009) introduced the concept of *strategic mentorship* that focused on mentoring, describing it as a series of focused strategic interactions with various individuals about specific professional issues (p. 1132). The process of rising to the executive level begins usually at a lower level position. The dream of rising to the executive suite will not and cannot be attained solely by an individual's own actions or strength.

Mentor's Role in Getting Promotion

"Ralph" viewed his opportunities as a result of aligning with the right leaders in the organization:

> Really maintaining a mentor relationship
> with the VP of HR of the organization, who
> ended up being a strong champion for me in
> the organization, was a key contributor to
> my success.

"Henry" viewed his strategies for promotion as intentional in his approach to securing a mentor. He was also proactive in making his presence known to those who were in decision making capacities. But he cautioned on being authentic or non-manipulative with the leader:

> I identify folks that appear to be very
> judicial and non-biased. I align myself with

them making my capabilities known to these folks and get involved in strategic projects that are highly visible relative to things that they influence...... in these peoples area of influence and turn it on and just own it and just blast through it, to the point that...... in other words the key decision-makers is in the vicinity at a particular point in time and just really own it, not from a manipulative point of view, but from working your ass off and making sure they are aware of the work you are doing..... publicize it....work through these people, through these people, make them look good, and then make it known I'm not just doing this for my good health.

"Edward" discussed how promotions occurred and reviewed the difficulty of attaining a mentor and having the organization actually support his career progression. He also mentioned the phenomenon of being the only one,

In retrospect I just don't think that was part our culture at the time, it wasn't part of the culture for me; I happen to be one out of 30 plus managers always the only African-American that was there. It was just really difficult back then trying to establish relationships and mentorships and coaches from the perspective of people really giving it to me straight, giving me the feedback, letting me know what or how I should be

thinking and showing up…very little of that,
so I really had to rely upon external sources
as a way to get that input.

"Jason's" mentioned the importance of networking and
why it was important for his career development to be
connected with the right people:

> I also focused on networking with people
> that were in decision-making positions that
> would have some input into whether or not
> if I were able to receive a promotion. I
> established my network by learning the
> culture of the organization I was in and I
> made sure that I interfaced with the people
> that were influential in the whole
> advancement planning or promotion
> process, starting with my immediate
> supervisor.

"Gary" also discussed the connection between not just
having a mentor or an enabler but also the importance of
individual performance,

> Networking was key and I insured my
> performance was there, I also had sponsors
> that enabled me to achieve the next level, I
> also had endorsers based upon the
> recommendation of my sponsors. I used
> brown bag lunches with other leaders that
> allowed me to talk to other leaders and
> express my desires as well as articulate my
> abilities. At the end of the lunch I would ask

for the leader to explain how they got
promoted.

Mentor's Role in Reaching Senior Management Positions

"James" described his journey to senior management and
felt leadership had a vested interest in him and wanted to
see him succeed:

> if you do not have leadership support the
> opportunity will not come to fruition, I
> really feel that someone had a vested interest
> in me and they said I should have that job
> and if that does not happen for an individual
> then the person is not going to get the
> job…it just doesn't happen like that…that's
> why people leave the organization…you
> have to have a voice behind you in
> succession planning meetings to be
> successful. I had a lot of supporters and
> mentors and they put my name on the table
> when promotable opportunities stood out.
> Anybody that thinks that they have done
> well simply because they were smart has the
> wrong impression.

Mentor's Role in Training Programs and Development of Skills

"Alfred" felt he had the fortune of management reaching
out to him and viewed this as an opportunity to increase his
leadership skills, enabling him to grow from level to level.

Management called me and told me that
they saw potential in me and sent me to a
leadership seminar because of the potential
they saw in me. It enabled me the
opportunity to increase my leadership skills
which helped me to grow from level to
level.

"Scott's" response centered on coaching and how his
manager became directly involved with his progression and
coached him in areas he could improve.

My manager recommended that I have
contacts with…in the organization my
manager thought there was a need for me to
be a lot more polished in presentations with
the CEO and those types of things…. He
recommended a course that would help me
hone in on those skills that would balance
my presentation skills where I didn't just talk
from the position of strength all the time, I
kept it even keel from there…he
recommended a consultant…that I talk to
him on monthly basis or quarterly basis to
make certain that I wasn't reverting back to
my own comfort zone.

Step 4: Be Performance-Driven

Tip 4, another major theme in interviewees' responses, was
the conviction that "I must perform." Performance is the
key to success regardless of race, creed or color.
Organizations strive to employ individuals who afford them

the best opportunity to succeed, and when employees succeed they are rewarded for their performance. Longenecker and Fink (2008) conducted a study on management promotional decisions and reported,

> Of the respondents, 77% view the number one factor for getting promoted is a person's ability to get results and generate a strong track record of performance. Managers made it clear that being a high performer over a period of time and getting results was the single most important factor in the promotion equation. (p. 243)

This emphasis on performance was certainly confirmed in the interviewees' personal experiences in their executive ascension. Many African Americans grow up being taught they have to be better than their European American counterparts, and that performing equal or less than European Americans would never propel them ahead in their life. This performance-driven mindset was evident in all of the ten executives I interviewed, and they acknowledge this attitude to be crucial in their success.

Performance-Driven Attitude in Getting Promotion

"James" felt he had to be better than the next person, and he couldn't be as good as the next person and still get promoted. That was his personal philosophy.

> Being "as good as" is average you have to be better, and if you are ok with good then you probably won't be as successful…. I

wanted to create a reputation of equality for everyone and not particular to other groups.

"Henry" indicated some people recognized his work in his organization, but maybe not at the right level. He also explained a situation where he was performing above the call of duty and had to engage management to recognize his work,

had folks that were willing to recognize the work that I had done and they would say man this is pretty good work, dude you need to be operating at a higher level. In one particular case, my first promotion at my current company I was actually doing two jobs and I just called it out that I'm doing two jobs here and unless you are going to add two level 28's and make me a level 56 then something's gotta happen here, so we just called it out like that and you got promoted. The other times that this has happened was really due to the fact that I was really doing some bang up work on high-profile projects and owning it in a singular way where you can create something that no one else has done before, not just doing the same thing that everybody else has done and doing it faster, harder and better, doing something that is not easily replicatable.

"Alfred" realized performing in the role you are in is the best way to be recognized and progress through the organization.

> First strategy is to perform in the job where you are at, be extraordinary in the role you are in. Find areas that I have transferrable skills to enhance performance. Early in my career I would do more to understand the requirements of a job and not go blindly into the role. Later in my career I would focus on a higher level of understanding of strategy where the organization is trying to go.... I performed in every job I was in, I'm a quick learner and was able to link plans and tactics with strategy and have outperformed the requirements of the role.

"Scott" took initiative to learn all he could to position himself for future opportunities, even if it was in a different area than the one for which he was responsible.

> When I started out as a manufacturing supervisor over a department I would learn all that I could learn about that particular department and then I would broaden my horizons to learn more about another department even though it was not a department that I may specifically supervise. I would still learn the goings on about what the activities of that particular department would be and that in itself

enabled me to be in position to be
promoted.

"Edward" indicated he was in a situation where mentors
were not afforded to him but he continued to perform and
seek out opportunities on his own. The ability to never give
up and keep pushing outside of his comfort zone enabled
his success.

> Promotions occurred by me seeking them
> out, keeping my ear to the ground if you
> will, about openings….about who was
> looking for people to do special projects,
> things of that sort, that was primarily how
> that worked. This may be out of order
> [interview sequence] but in terms of the
> training, promotions, and jobs that I have
> had conferred upon me, there was no real
> mentors or coaches internally, a lot of the
> advice, career advice I received came from
> external sources.

"Gary" regularly met with sponsors and asked what their
keys to success were and also mentioned that above
networking, he had to perform.

> I also had sponsors that enabled me to
> achieve the next level; I also had endorsers
> based upon the recommendation of my
> sponsors. I used brown bag lunches with
> other leaders that allowed me to talk to other
> leaders and express my desires as well as
> articulate my abilities. At the end of the

lunch I would ask for the leader to explain
on how they got promoted. I also found that
working out in the gym produced favorable
reactions and opportunities for me…other
leaders were in the gym and it allowed them
to see me in a different light. But
performance is always first and foremost.

"Marquis" discussed his approach of self-analysis to secure
promotion, which he clarified should not be extended to the
point of self-effacing, but really being in touch with his
own strengths and opportunities. His ability to self-assess
left a lasting impact on his management team:

So I would walk in and I would actually be
more critical of myself than they would,
because I knew where I wanted to go and
there were a couple of times where I would
go in for my review in front of the partner
and he would say, —gosh you're being
tough on yourself‖, I would say no here's the
reality this is where I want to go, I know
what I want to be, I know what I want to
accomplish, and if I'm not accomplishing
that I'll be the first one to say it. I employed
a perspective of being self-critical in being
more critical of myself than anyone else
could be and I didn't do that for reverse
psychology perspective but because I knew
where I wanted to go and if I wasn't
progressing in that manner, I wasn't

accomplishing those goals, to me I wasn't doing myself justice.

Performance-Driven Attitude in Career Path

"Jason" mentioned the need to perform well in the role you are in, as opposed to worrying about the next role, indicating that performance in the current role is the key to the next role,

> My approach was trying to be prepared for the next position by performing well in the position I was in currently or held at the time, in other words executing the existing position well, learning all the nuances of the position, and preparing to take the next steps in moving up in terms of responsibility. That implies getting the right education whether it is formal or informal to be effective in the position.

"Robert" indicated his career path approach focused on image portrayal and performance as the keys to success. He also mentioned how influence in the organization assisted him:

> Top of mind it was working hard and demonstrating my capabilities to do more and performing at a high level. My approach changed as I went higher in the organization... It was about leadership, strategic capabilities and the ability to influence throughout the organization. Early

on it's about the image you portray. If you want to be at the executive level or the C-Suite, then you need to carry yourself that way.

Step 5: Ownership in Performance Reviews

Expressing ownership in performance reviews is the fifth theme in the ten executives' stories. It's essentially an attitude that says or conveys, "I own it," or "It was my responsibility." Performance reviews are essential to effective succession-planning and talent-management programs within corporations, and fruitful performance reviews result from this ownership attitude.

Wilbanks (2011) encourages employees owning the performance review process, stating,

> One of the worst aspects of a manager's job is writing performance reviews. It's easy to review the top performers–just tell them that they're doing great and give them their well–deserved bonuses. But what about the middle performers or those who need improvement? How does an effective manager write and discuss a review that will encourage improvement? It all starts with the employee self-assessment. (p. 58)

And most certainly, all ten executives I interviewed repeatedly claimed ownership of the self-assessment process. By requesting a self-assessment, the manager has empowered the employee to guide and direct the review.

Employees who take the process seriously will benefit from the lack of management focus as the worker can dictate the tone of the review. Employees who approach the review haphazardly are left to their own contrivance. Below are the executives' responses regarding the performance review process, who leads the process, if there are any surprises in the process, and how the surprises are resolved if there were.

"Ralph's" experience:

> I should be checking in on my progress on how I'm tracking to the goals set for myself and agreed to. We should talk about that twice a year and if I'm derailing or if someone who is working for me is derailing, then it should be more often than that. In my experience my training has told me that effective performance management you don't have an annual performance review that is an absolute shock or surprise to the individual that is receiving that review.

"James'" experience:

> You should have ongoing dialogue every two weeks, once a month, weekly, to ensure that surprises don't happen. You don't want issues to arise in the 11th hour about a situation that needs to be resolved and be more proactive than reactive.

"Henry's" experience:

The way it's supposed to work is you fill out your own assessment of your performance over the course of the year against your objectives that you have laid out in front of you and then you get together with your manager at the midyear to a checkpoint to see how you are progressing and then at the same time at the end of the year. You don't have quarterly reviews but you expect your manager…. I always personally inquired how it was going, this is what I'm supposed to be indexing against, from your point of view and perspective what's the progress you're seeing against it, because I don't like surprises.

"Alfred's" experience:

First I try to identify my strengths and weaknesses, the performance review is a key component also and I also use 360 to help provide a broader perspective of my performance. I also use 1:1 feedback with managers to get additional feedback and then develop an action plan to improve my performance and focus on 3-5 items…be honest with yourself, are you capable of doing the role…understanding the culture…can you be successful in the position?

"Scott's" experience:

> When we didn't have a more formalized
> process in place, it was always subjective,
> from the standpoint yeah costs were down
> but you didn't have five meetings with your
> direct plant manager…those types of
> things….You could've had four meetings or
> three meetings with them but that's not
> something we could measure or anything.
> This is something that you bring up as a
> talking point, where once a process was in
> place, where you knew what your goals
> were and you and the manager agreed
> upon…this is what we're working on, along
> with the resources you need…then let's go.

"Edward's" experience:

> I know that the expectation is that
> performance is reviewed quarterly so it
> really is up to me to kinda marshal that
> interaction

"Jason's" experience:

> I remember specifically one time, probably
> in the middle of my career, that I was up for
> promotion that I thought I should've gotten
> and most my peers thought I should've got
> it. In my review my supervisor came up with
> a very minor point that he used to really
> disqualify me from the promotion and it was
> a surprise because it really had no substance

to it at all and it surprised me because it's more of a factor just to disqualify me, it was a surprise. I didn't think it was significant at all. He and I had a very frank conversation about it and I made sure that it was completely understood on both parts what the element was that we were discussing to resolve in that meeting so that it would not come up in the future. It was a very frank face-to-face and heated conversation.

"Gary's" experience:

I would write my own performance review for the review process. This allowed me to explain what the performance was and positioned me to have more impact in the review because I better understood the situation…informally I was sitting down with my manager every 90 days. Formally the process was two times per year.

"Robert's" experience:

I had one manager throughout my career that I would say was poor at performance reviews, and I let him know that. He was poor at doing performance reviews; we met at a bar because he didn't take it seriously. At that same meeting he rated me a Good and he knew I was disappointed and that this was unacceptable, I also knew at that time I no longer wanted to work for him any longer and I spoke with another manager and he told me to hang in there. And then I was moved over to another manager and eventually was this guy's peer, within a year. I was very straight up with people; as long as you are performing you can be respectful. You have to be honest with yourself and you gotta be honest with the people around you. The other thing I would tell you is it really is incumbent upon the employee to make sure that they have the right performance and process, the manager has to participate, but the employee needs to work with the manager to set the time up in getting things done, it's a two-way street. If you have a poor manager then you have to work with him and work a little harder to make those things happen. I used to have employees write the review up and I would look at it and we will talk through it and I would get it in advance of them doing the review. I would be prepared and have questions, my notes throughout the year, write in the areas where they improved and they also did the same thing. Also capturing their overarching strengths and development needs and we would talk through that and have a conversation to really find out what was what.

"Marquis'" experience:

In general it has been a partner [who
conducted the review], I've probably only
had one time in one practice where it was
not a partner, as far as leading the process
goes it is an interactive process in that they
gave you a self-performance evaluation, you
fill that out and turned it in and you kept a
copy. If you are smart you walked in with a
copy and you went down the list and made it
an interactive session. I'm sure there are
people that didn't do it that way, but that's
the way I did it.

Step 6: White Female Colleagues – Understand Their Impact on Your Career

The sixth theme that emerged from the ten interviewed
executives is the impact of white female colleagues on their
executive ascension. It is critical that African American
men be aware of and ready for this factor in their journey
into the executive suite.

In 1984, Hambrick and Mason discussed three areas in
which perceptual process was influenced: (a) a
management team cannot scan every aspect of the company
environment; (b) the managers' perceptions are limited
because they perceive only the phenomena in their view;
and (c) the bits of information chosen are filtered by the
individuals' cognitive base and values. All three points
provide solid indications of why African American men are
not proportionally represented within organizations because
hiring managers will say they cannot scan or recognize all
employees, their perceptions of talent are limited to the

group that they are familiar, which is typically fellow White men and the filtering process allows them to see what they want to see.

The participants described an additional concern with the perceptual process as they indicated African American men are passed over for promotions as white women are seen as an alternative choice to African American men. The perception of the four African American participants is supported by the observation from Peterson, Philpot, and O'Shaughnessy (2007) as they indicated African American men are third in the pecking order of corporate structures with the preferred order focused on white men and white women. In the course of the interviews, four of the ten participants mentioned their experiences of white women gaining preference in promotional opportunities.

"James'" recollection of his company's success of increasing diversity representation, and stated:

> [White] women have succeeded in this area because there is a certain comfort level with [white] women over POC (people of color) and the perspective is not always balanced because of the level of familiarity.

"Henry" experienced being passed over for a promotion in lieu of a white woman:

> There were two jobs… I had one of them and they're trying to bring another lady in to be my counterpart in from a field position and at the same time I had my eye on

another promotion and I was told that we don't have any money to promote you to this job but, in fact I found out from a colleague who had visibility to it and said not only were they going to have money to promote somebody, they were going to actually throw incentive money at this individual to get her to take the job, which was the same job that I was in. So basically I'm asking you something and you are telling me you don't have it, but you're doing all this other stuff for a Caucasian woman, so it was a bald face lie.

"Edward" also experienced being passed over because of a white female colleague.

We had a really decent relationship and I would get reviewed annually, it was like a one-time kind of deal we sat down and actually talked about performance and I had all the requirements for this project manager job, but I'll never forget a conversation I had with the CIO, he actually told me that he needed me to wait, that there were some other things coming down the pipe, but there was this [white] woman that had been recommended and he really needed to bring her into the organization and the way that he could her bring in was in this open project manager position.

"Jason" also had a similar experience.

> In my organization diversity as a whole was defined as promoting white women. If you look at diversity in terms of the makeup of people in the advancement planning pool for example you see that women advance more rapidly than other people in the organization because it's easier as people have the tendency to accept what's closer to being like them and in that case there'd been a move towards a white women because women are growing in the numbers in the organization and it's easier to promote the women than people of color throughout the organization.

Step 7: Never Give Up

The seventh and last theme, appropriately, is that there are no easy roads to success in the interviewees' executive ascension. They worked hard and made many sacrifices along the way. Longenecker and Fink (2008) observed, "The demands on mangers have never been greater and they have never faced more challenges. Many manages who were previously successful in more staid environments are not able to keep up or perform effectively in this environment" (p. 249). Some of the sacrifices that my interviewees made included moving from one location to another or taking a position that did not seem within the realm of their career progression. Whatever the difficulty, all of their experiences converge on one point: the journey is difficult, but never give up because success is possible.

Difficulties in Career Path? Never Give Up

"Ralph" acknowledged having to take different paths in developing his career.

> It's really been about trying to round out my career in human resources, from a generalist perspective I was able to gain various experiences by going to different divisions within the organization. I started out in the manufacturing HR role, then took a detour into the HR systems role, at that point I had some specialist experience and I had champions in the organization that would be looking out for my career as well.

"Henry" considered his career path approach and viewed his path as nontraditional and indicated his climb on the corporate ladder was different because of a decentralized selling organization.

> I've known for a long time that the only way up in this organization is to spend multiple tours of duty coming through the corporate office. The traditional path has been come in and do a stint, go back out, come back in, go back out and I haven't done that at all. To a certain extent I have actually played a hand in limiting my upward mobility in this organization because I do not want to go into the corporate office. Where I've had opportunities to shine and display well... capable of doing... I recognize those

opportunities when I had sponsors in the building and I usually just put on it blast at that particular point in time and would try to speed pass, to use an analogy, it's like a situation where it's like one of those promotions where they put you in an air chamber and we are going to blow money up and as much money you can grab in 60 seconds, go! That type of thing…. that feels kind of like what I've done in a couple situations where I've had the right people at the right place, at the right time in lieu of going in and going into the building, and just kinda grinding it out, it's been a conscious decision. I look at it and I say can I be further with my company than where I am right now, yes absolutely, but the key is the fact that I decided there are certain things that I don't want to do and I am responsible for where I am in part today because of those decisions.

"Scott" described taking a career path less traveled today.

I would describe my career path approach being one of what would be considered uncharacteristic, old-school today, which I started at low level and then I worked my way up to the level where I would always ask for increasing amounts of responsibility. I would always strive through either knowledge or education or external ways to

learn as much as I could about the
organization that I work for and target
specific positions that I felt that I had the
ability and skills to lead.

Difficulties in Getting Promoted? Never Give Up

"James" shared his struggle with getting a promotion.

> I felt I would never be recognized on an
> equal basis with equal performance…. I had
> to be above and beyond. If I was going to be
> measured against others, it had to be obvious
> to the managers that I was better otherwise I
> was not going to make it.

"Jason" described the hard, cold, unexpected reality that
you could encounter in any business, which is the first and
last thing companies care about is performance,

> There are two keys, number one,
> performance, you have to perform, in
> business you really have to perform they
> really don't care if you're black, white, or
> green, they're looking for you to get the job
> done and who performs. One of the things
> that I try to specialize in was taking on some
> of the…or taking on the tough assignments,
> the ones that are high risk and high reward,
> and I was successful at doing some of those
> and I got the awards to demonstrate that.

"Robert" advocated knowing what you want and
developing steps to get there are critical to forward

progression. In addition to the performance requirement, he discussed having the knowledge of how the organization works as a critical component to success,

> I didn't play games; my process was being straight up. I was a high performer. Now in my career everything didn't always go well and I'm sure that is a question you are going to ask later. One of the things I did was I marked a mental *x* at a point where there was a need for improvement or failure and ensure to myself that I would not duplicate the same mistake nor allow this to happen again. I tried to never blame the person for what happened to me, I took full responsibility.

Difficulties All Around? Never Give Up

"Alfred" reflected that he would have recognized things are not always what they seem and he needed to understand the role thoroughly before he got into it. He cautioned,

> First focus on the tactical and operational requirements and second understand the strategy…be honest with yourself are you capable of doing the role? Understanding the culture, can you be successful in the position?

"Gary" remembered having to learn a lesson he wish he had learned early in his career, which is the ability to know when it was time to move on to the next opportunity.

I became stagnated at the last level prior to becoming executive and started to realize that I needed to start looking for other opportunities. I had been recruited by other companies, but did not entertain them, but once I realized the executive level was not going to be attained I then started listening to offers as they came in. I would have been more aggressive in following up and not just having my head down. I spoke of the biggest miss of African Americans was not focusing on career development and networking and following up. I was taught that if you did a good job then your work would be recognized.

"Marquis" responded to the question about skill development and growth in an organization, stressing that either you know you are good or you are not, and once you figure out where you stand your next steps are a little easier to navigate,

Either you're good at it or you're not, when you're not good at it most of those practices would let you know and you took a different pathway than say somebody who wasn't good at it. I happen to be relatively good at, not only be a meticulous and fairly good designer, but I was also good at talking with clients and actually going out and meeting people and conducting meetings and things like that. I had a fairly good cross-section of what we call a holistic architect; a holistic architect is a guy who has to wear many hats in order to do what we do. If you cannot do that then we kinda stay on the technical side as opposed to the management side or if you're not very good technically…used in the management side as opposed to technical side, but there were some of us who were right in the middle and those are the ones who usually become partner, those are the ones who usually become sole proprietors and start their own practice.

Now that you are armed with the 7 tips for success, PINDOWN, which have contributed to the success of these ten executives, you should have a good profile of an ambitious and competent professional. In the next chapter, I will outline further suggestions offered by these ten interviewees.

CHAPTER 5

Further Advice for Filling the African American Void

My interviews with the ten African American male executives were enlightening and encouraging – enlightening because there were universal themes present in all of their experiences that could serve others to succeed also, encouraging because success *is* possible despite all the obstacles standing in the way. Besides the seven universal themes, the ten successful executives offered other tips and advice that will help you along on this journey.

This phenomenological study, which focused on the lived experiences of the ten interviewees of the phenomenon of executive ascension, yielded valuable insight into the process of attaining senior-level management positions. Though they represented various organizations and industries, the executives had a shared story that can be your own roadmap. For those already occupying the executive chair, these can be helpful advice for your company to expand its diversity and prepare its talent pipeline for succession planning.

These further tips are presented according to three categories: talent management, succession planning, and diversity practices.

Talent Management

Know the System and Process of Succession Planning

All but one of the interviewees ("Edward") expressed that they were knowledgeable of the succession-planning process in their organization. Many indicated the process had a name and an acronym, which are omitted to protect the identity of the participants. The interviewees described this process as the time to review high-potentials and the process for filling the pipeline.

Cantrell and Benton (2007) found that "few organizations regularly undertake measurement and feedback-based improvement; indeed, executives at about half the organizations we surveyed reported that they never or seldom did" (p. 359). In the same study, they found that 23% of employees surveyed do not think HR policies are clear, fair and consistent. When communication like this left much to be desired, employees who try to understand their organizations with intentionality can succeed, like the interviewed executives.

In some cases, however, organizations do communicate to their employees about how the system works. "Marquis" stated, "Within our profession we have a very strict, specific program that you have to go through in order to become a licensed architect professional," indicating clear understanding of the process. "Edward" also stated, "It's very clear and laid out what the career paths are and the requirements for those career paths."

An organization should strive to create an information-sharing environment, which can foster talent development and prepare the right employees for senior management positions down the road. Cantrell and Benton (2007) indicated, "Surprisingly, only 35 percent of the organizations in our study report achieving even moderate success in maintaining knowledge repositories; the remaining 65 percent report that they never or seldom update their knowledge management systems" (p. 362). Having an information-sharing environment directly addresses the mystery of succession planning that some of the participants mentioned in their interviews. For organizations to improve their talent and address the current talent shortage, informing employees and leadership on the process of talent evaluation can create better employee engagement and increase retention rates of high potential employees.

Be Willing to Step Out of Your Comfort Zone and/or Relocate

To obtain executive positions, an employee must perform his best and be willing to take on unfamiliar tasks. Cartwright (2008) indicates that employees must be able to demonstrate their ability to prioritize their work or be labeled as incompetent or a person unable to manage complex tasks. "Jason" confirmed this, saying that when hiring people, "I looked for work performance, meaning how dependable is that person, are they the kind of person that will spend the extra time, are they meticulous in a profession like mine?"

It is not enough to deliver impressive results in your given role; in order to advance in an organization; many of my interviewees had to step outside of their comfort zone. "Scott" recounted, "I would go through strategic planning exercises and look into areas and ways that I could better my skills as a strategic planner." "Robert" also stated, "One thing I would tell you is that individuals need to be proactive in terms of their own development; they have to own their career and own their development."

White (2006) also indicated an organization needs to understand who the key players are on the team and designate them with priority rankings of A, B or C. Team members designated as A players were deemed as exceptional individuals, B players were viewed as steady and consistent individuals, whereas C players were perceived to be individuals that blocked the pipeline due to their inconsistent performance. The concept of categorizing employees correlated to the aforementioned concept of particular value. Particular value is being applied when an employee is designated as an A player and their opportunities of training and advancement are more than the B or C player. The issue with designating any employee deals with the perceived value or contribution of the individual.

The participants of this study clearly recognized when the concept of particular value was being applied to them and conversely forced them to step outside of their comfort zone. "Gary" commented, "Those that had great connections were promoted, but if others were less aggressive, then they did not get as much support." The participants have certainly added a critical component to talent-management that aligns with the proactive and intentional themes previously discussed.

Another way to express your willingness to step outside of the comfort zone is to be willing to relocate. Although relocation and its benefits for career advancement are not the focus of this book or my doctoral research, my interviewees certainly reported relocation as a contributing factor to their upward mobility.

Allen, Eby, Douthitt, and Noble (2002) indicated employees who move for new positions enjoy increased positions and wages within their company, as compared to employees who are not as receptive to moving. Only two of the interviewees did not relocate in order to advance in their organization. Within organizations for upward movement to occur an employee needs to be flexible regarding locations or they have the potential to limit their career progression. "Henry" admitted, "To a certain extent I have actually played a hand in limiting my upward mobility in this organization because I do not want to go to into the corporate office."

Allen et al. indicated the ability to relocate has positive and negative benefits and requires trade-offs for the individual and his family. The trade-offs include selling your home, cost of living adjustments, children in school and spousal support. The added concern for African American men and their families is being relocated into a dense population of European Americans with very few people of their own persuasion in the neighborhood. There is no right or wrong answers and the decision hinged on the preferences of the individual. However, as "Henry" related, when you do not relocate, then you are likely to limit your upward mobility.

"Gary" discussed his a hard decision about relocation and how he handled it: "In one role I did not relocate but commuted because my child was still in school…I was upfront about my ability to not relocate and commute and the company was open to my request." "Robert" added, "I had several discussions with people and didn't want to take my kids out of school, nor did I want to commute, I let people know what was important to me."

Relocation can be put you in position for the next key advancement, and African Americans should openly communicate their position on relocation and understand the impact the decision may have on reaching the executive suite.

Own Your Career Path

The interviewees indicated personal ownership of their careers was the key to progression from level to level. All of them received promotions, with several reaching double-digits in the number of times they were promoted. In discussing how they approached their career path planning, all interviewees indicated they had a solid understanding of their career path and they made deliberate actions to elevate themselves in their respective organizations. "Robert" stated, "Top of mind it was working hard and demonstrating my capabilities to do more and performing at a high level." "Scott" added, "I would learn all that I could learn about a particular department and then I would broaden my horizons to learn more about another department."

Altman (2009) discussed the talent-management process and reviewed internal versus external candidates and stated,

> There are advantages in bringing in a
> successor designate with wide relevant
> experience, but there is much to be said too
> for a homegrown candidate who understands
> the culture and dynamics of the business and
> shows a strong degree of loyalty. (p. 72)

Altman's point of homegrown talent should not fall on deaf ears. Considerable discussion has taken place regarding the participants approach to managing their careers. In many cases the interviewees have been resilient in reaching the executive suite and have gone to great lengths to overcome the obstacles they have encountered. Altman addresses the opportunity to develop homegrown talent as opposed to bringing in outside leadership. The interviewees claimed ownership of the process, but the ownership should not solely rely upon them to be successful. Organizational leadership is also responsible in ensuring employee success.

The concern with talented employees conducting their own training or searching for advancement opportunities is the practice may ultimately lead them to another organization rendering a void in the departed organization. Altman (2009) viewed a critical lesson to be learned by corporations is to begin the talent management process early because talent is scarce and the good ones will find opportunities elsewhere.

All of the interviewees were actively involved in their organizations' talent-management process that enabled them to achieve various promotions. An additional action the participants took was their willingness to relocate for opportunities, eight of the ten interviewees relocated for advancement opportunities that helped them to advance in their career. "Robert" stated, "I had conversations with people high in the organization before positions came up in terms of what things I wanted in my career and found out where I stood with people." Knowing where you stand is critical for career progression; you cannot leave your progression to chance or unfounded hope that someone is looking out for you.

Succession Planning

Fegley (as cited in Barnett and Davis, 2008) indicated 58% of respondents from a recent study communicated their organization had some level of succession-planning, leaving 42% of organizations that did not have a succession-planning process or were planning to implement a process. Having a succession-planning process is critical to filling the talent pipeline, without the process organizations are at risk of not having the talent in place when needed. This section unfolds the mystery of placement, with the interviewees helping to shed light on who is involved, how the process works, and when the decisions are made.

Formalized Mentoring

Although the interviewees indicated mentoring was a big factor in the succession-planning process, some were not afforded mentors in their organizations. "Alfred" indicated,

> The company does have a formalized process but I have not been introduced to it, still new to the organization. My previous organization had a database for employees to be entered into the process and individuals were assigned to a mentor.

"Gary" described his experience with mentorship: "My current company yes, previous companies not as much. It was more of an informal process. People were not assigned mentors and this was irrespective of gender and race." But mentorship is crucial; those who had mentors prospered, and those who did not have mentors did not prosper. "James" stated, "I believe that people are successful because someone wants to see them succeed."

But it's not enough to just have anyone. "Robert" and "Ralph" recalled unproductive mentorship experiences in their journey, where there was a lack of chemistry or rapport in a forced mentorship match. The key lesson is to connect mentees and mentors whose personalities and goals are aligned.

Besides providing an environment where informal mentoring could occur, organizations should also consider implementing formalized mentoring. Cingoranelli (2009) indicated that nurturing future leaders was a key to effective succession planning. Mentoring is a form of nurturing and, if done right, can produce positive results for the organization. Mentoring proved to be a useful tool for my interviewees. Only one interviewee indicated his organization did not have a formal or informal mentoring process. The distinction between a formal and an informal mentoring process is the designation of the mentee by management.

In addition to nurturing future leaders, formal mentoring is key to the retention of women and minority executives, according to Greer and Virick (2008). Formal mentoring not only helps employees develop skills, it can also be a process in which hidden messages in the organization's culture can be relayed to employees. "Ralph" stated, "Basically you had leaders in the HR structure of VPs and above who were tapped and told that they would receive a mentee and they would be selected for them."

Mentoring also allows for an added level of understanding and knowledge-sharing to take place, observed Greer and Virick (2008). In a woman-to-woman mentoring relationship, the nuances of being a woman in the workplace can be better explained than by a male mentor. The same consideration applies for a minority being mentored by another minority employee who understands the challenges of being a minority employee.

Communication of Senior Management Positions

Owens and Young (2008) found that "60%–75% of job openings are never advertised publicly but are found through the hidden job market" (p. 23). They advocated networking as a critical tool that enables employees to gain organizational advancement, echoing the adage "It is not who you are, but who you know, that takes center stage in networking." The topic of networking is worthy of further examination, but it was not a focus of this study. The key take-away is the importance of knowing the right people, because you may not otherwise know of vacant positions.

Nine of the ten interviewees said that senior positions were not communicated within their organizations, further confirming that the availability of senior management positions remains a mystery in many companies. "James" stated,

> Many times open jobs are [communicated] but the candidates are already determined. The candidates are identified during the succession planning. The opportunity has to be relevant. Some candidates are not included because the organization does not want them to be.

"Alfred" stated,

> No, typically you find out by word of mouth. First level VPs are posted on the job board and that is probably the only communication of senior management level positions. Most positions are managed through the succession-planning process and not broadly communicated.

"Henry" confirmed,

So it's not really like….. look I've got this
VP job open just throw your name in the hat.
Then one smoky, shadowy, mysterious day,
they're over in that room, the one that
doesn't have a number on it or a knob on the
door….. that's where it seems like they
already have their master plan and unless
you have admittance to that room, then you
are pretty much shaded out from what
happens. That sounds terrible, like a victim's
mentality, but honestly that's been my
observation that seems to be the way things
work here.

The message is clear: organizations prefer to keep the
succession-planning process a mystery and the knowledge
is only shared with a close knit group of leaders. However,
"Jason" offers advice for getting into the process,

The whole thing about advancement
planning or succession planning is to make
it work…it works for those people who are
most knowledgeable of the corporate culture
and who have the formal and informal
mentors. The average person that does not
have a plan or design won't know the details
of an advancement plan in our organization
and in most organizations.

Dutton (2009) found that most companies do not conduct
any career or succession planning and consequently, when
an employee leaves the organization, the company is not
prepared to manage the departure. Careers can be destroyed

for lack of knowledge. Not knowing how the succession-planning process works and what talent-management programs are afforded to individuals can doom careers. The mystery of senior level positions can be revealed, but it will take intentional actions from participants to discover the process.

Performance Review Process

All interviewees agreed that performance reviews were the linchpin to succession. Some had performance reviews on an annual basis, while others underwent the reviews more frequently, semi-annually or quarterly.

"James" identified two critical processes of the performance review. First, an employee cannot lead the process; second, an employee has to ensure he is part of the process. The remaining participants clarified the ownership aspect of performance reviews process, rather than leaving the process up to their manager to administer. The consensus from the participants was the employee is provided with an opportunity to self-assess their performance and then the manager meets with the employee to discuss performance and communicate a performance rating.

The theme from the interviewees' response regarding performance review is that, in order for the review to be effective, the employee and the manager need to be aligned on performance metrics and have regular conversations regarding performance. Without alignment and consistent conversation, the year-end rating could present some surprises. It is not uncommon for there to be surprises in a performance review discussion for a myriad of reasons.

To avoid such "surprises" that result from miscommunication, misunderstanding, or any other reason, my interviewees recommended the following:

☐ Get a coach or a mentor ("Edward")

☐ Understand the process ("Alfred")

☐ Make sure the goals are not subjective ("Scott")

☐ Set the stage for your expectations in the performance review ("Robert")

☐ Get constant feedback–weekly, monthly ("James")

☐ Do not be afraid to have frank conversations if there is disagreement ("Jason")

☐ If there is disagreement, get it on the record ("Henry")

☐ Do not be surprised ("Ralph")

☐ Manage the manager with 90 day check points ("Gary")

☐ Accountability–be the first one to hold your hand up if something goes wrong ("Marquis")

While performance reviews are key to career advancement, sometimes this is a process that managers don't take very seriously. The consensus of the interviewees was that the employee owns the performance review process and an employee should not go into a performance review without his own list of accomplishments. The process is typically administered on a mid-year and full-year basis. The employee completes a self-assessment and sends the assessment to their respective manager and the manager then assigns a rating.

Several participants reported their managers did a really poor job executing the performance review. "Robert" speaks of a less-than-spectacular review he received from his manager at a bar where his manager attempted to complete the review over a beer. "Henry" felt the whole performance review process was arbitrary although it was supposed to be the deciding factor on what salary treatments were going to be. One year "Henry" had to submit salary increases prior to even completing the employee assessment, so when the actual reviews were completed they were anticlimactic.

Therefore, given the importance of performance reviews and the unpredictable attitude of the managers, all interviewees agreed they had to take ownership of the process in order to achieve a satisfactory outcome. They never left it to chance. They made recommendations on how to prepare for the performance review: (a) have a list of your accomplishments, (b) conduct quarterly manager meetings, (c) ensure the discussion is a two-way dialogue and not a monologue of the manager only providing his perspective, and (d) make sure goals are agreed upon at the beginning of the year and confirm alignment on the metrics.

If there are any surprises at the end of the year in a performance review, ask to increase the frequency of performance discussions, have a frank conversation with your manager to gain better understanding for the future.

Coaching: Development of Future Leaders & Improvement of Individual Employee Performances

Berchelman (2005) expresses his love for the book *Hope is Not a Strategy* and comments, "We hope things don't happen, but sometimes they do, we hope for sunshine and plan for rain, such is the impetus for sound succession planning" (p. 11) The development of future leaders requires intentional actions from the developer and the developed. The development of future leaders requires parties to have a vested interest in the welfare of the individual and the company. Hoping that organizations have succession plans or hoping that they are effective is simply not enough.

However, McDermott et al. (2007) warned, "Ineffective coaching can lead to poor execution of business strategy and failed teamwork, reduced employee motivation and organization culture, along with poor communication and perceived management responsiveness" (p. 33). The development of future leaders will be difficult to accomplish if leaders do not lead employees effectively. Berchelman (2005) adds, "The lack of executive talent can have catastrophic impact on the business" (p. 11).

McDermott et al. (2007) discovered that when the objectives of the coaching process are not clear and the practice of coaching is done in order to make the employee feel good, the coaching process is not as successful. The coaching process should be about improvement, not a degrading process of communication. "Edward" recalled many of the coaching discussions were punitive in nature, focusing more on what did not happen rather than what needed to happen. "Jason" on the other hand described a more positive experience, "My supervisor would coach me and make available people that were knowledgeable in that area to help me gain the knowledge." His coaching experience was a moral support and a means of providing him with the tools to gain additional skills.

Another way in which unproductive coaching is manifested is unwarranted labeling of minorities by their coaches or mentors. Although the phenomenon of black rage was not prevalent in the experiences of my interviewees, "Gary" touched on this subject when he discussed his experience with receiving coaching. He remembered being told to be "less aggressive" or "less over-bearing." "Gary" said, "I found that minorities get flagged with the labels more than white guys, the one criticism that routinely comes up is I'm too aggressive, I always positioned things with a solution and found that the white guy would do the same thing and would be viewed as offering constructive criticism."

This labeling is an important topic to discuss because it speaks directly to the point made by McDermott et al. (2007) regarding ineffective coaching. The consequence of ineffective or counter-productive coaching is manifold:

poor execution of business strategy and failed teamwork, reduced employee motivation and organization culture, along with poor communication and perceived management responsiveness. Managers and other leaders should take a holistic approach to coaching their employees and not fall prey to stereotypical thinking.

Lastly, more impactful than receiving coaching is acting upon the coaching. McDermott et al. (2007) discussed that most executives are unaware of how to use a coach; they are only concerned with completing the coaching sessions. "Henry" provided insight into how he responded to receiving coaching, "It's not like a denial situation, I didn't say I don't know what you are talking about, I said I'm going to work on that and consequently, subconsciously it sits on my left shoulder all the time like a parrot."

Press On Despite Promotion Exclusion

Although all of the interviewees were already successful at the time of the interview, almost all had been excluded from promotional opportunities at an earlier point in their career and discovered the exclusion in various ways. "Ralph" thought he was being considered for a VP position and he did not learn he was not in the candidate pool until after the announcement of the person who received the role. "Henry" shared he was informed he did not get a promotion by a fellow employee, as opposed to his manager.

"Scott" had a particularly agonizing experience with promotion exclusion, when his manager lied to another manager about the level of his interest in the job:

I didn't feel too good, obviously, so I talked to my plant manager and he said he didn't know much about it either so we went up to the president's office, and he said I wanted you to stay here because I'm looking at promoting you here in this unit and I feel this to be more of a value for you to continue doing what you're doing here and work your way through the system as opposed to going there. Which this wasn't the answer that I wanted to hear, and it wasn't his position to make that assumption without talking to me or my immediate manager who knew that I was interested in any relocation opportunities, but it was just a situation where it was at the crossroads of my career where I was really thinking whether or not I wanted to stay with the company. I let the situation stew, I talked with my wife over it, I let the situation stew for a couple months just to see, let me back up a little bit…. he did indicate that the recent changes that he knew …..that were coming downstream that he felt I would be promoted to….. in that particular area and I said well I'll give it three months and if I don't see activity…..I will keep my ear to the grindstone and if I don't see anything happening then I'm going to think about moving on and fortunately there was activity

but it wasn't activity that the guy thought
because they got rid of him!

Being excluded is never a good feeling regardless of the situation or the topic. For succession plans to be effective, communication should be consistent and inclusive, or organizations will encounter retention problems.

Being excluded from an opportunity and later discovering the facts of the exclusion can have a demoralizing effect on an employee. However, even though situations did not work out the way the interviewees wanted, their internal fortitude enabled them to persevere and continue to press forward in their careers.

Diversity Practices

Though this study did not intend to identify the acceptance and practice of diversity as a key contributor to the success of African American men in the succession-planning process, the presence of diversity or lack thereof had an impact on the interviewees' careers. McVittie, McKinlay and Widdicombe (2008) understood diversity in the workplace to mean "the recruitment, retention, promotion and rewarding of a heterogeneous mix of individuals within an organization" (p. 349). Using this definition of diversity, eight of the ten interviewees agreed that their organizations had defined diversity, but the majority thought the diversity programs were ineffective.

"Henry" thought his organization's progress on diversity was discouraging: "They have panels of folks up front at a national sales meeting and when I look at this panel and I don't see anybody that looks like me, that does not give me a lot of encouragement." Garyl shared the sentiment, "The retention and promotion of diverse people was not as successful, a lot of training was done but it was because they had to because of government regulations or the company being afraid of lawsuits." "Jason" added, "On a scale of 1 to 10 the effectiveness rating would be a 5, because it met all of the legal criteria, had it been truly effective it would do more to change the culture of the organization."

The participants also commented on the hindrances to fielding a diverse organization. "Ralph" stated it best: "I think that comes from the top...in my mind I think that policies can drive that, I think that maybe informally different leaders on the business can be challenged with that and I just don't hear those conversations happening." The interviewees confirmed the conclusions of scholarly literature that leadership or improvement on diversity comes from the top-senior management of the organization, beginning with the Board of Directors (Morrison, Oladunjoye, & Rose, 2008).

To effectively change the corporate landscape, board leadership needs to be intentional in their hiring or appointing actions. Fairfax (2005) commented, "While women and people of color have experienced some increase in board representation over the last few decades, both groups also have encountered significant barriers to their success on corporate boards" (p. 1105). Singh (2007) stated, "Those responsible for recruiting directors seek particular characteristics in new appointees to complement the existing board and to provide connections to new resources to secure the future of the firm." If the particular characteristics only focus on those who look like fellow board members then the mirror image appointments continue and that has a negative influence on the organizations diversity.

Improving company diversity involves the trickledown effect; if the board of directors is diverse then mandates can be passed down to leadership. Many boards suffer from the mirror image concept as well, resulting in an organization that resembles the board and the board resembles the organization – usually white men. Nicolson and Newton (2010) indicated boards are responsible for overseeing risk, compliance, strategy, governance, developing the CEO and senior management and managing stakeholders. The board of directors has the ability to set objectives for the CEO and the company to achieve on an annual basis and there is a no reason why the board is not more active in the process of setting diversity goals.

The business adage, "What gets measured, gets focus", means if organizations really want to impact their diversity representation and not just offer rhetoric, then they should monetarily measure leaders on their diversity goals and watch behavior change. Diversifying the organization is not without merit. The buying habits of consumer are changing as are the demographics. Organizations that hire and promote talented, diverse individuals will be better positioned to create strategies and products to meet the demands of the changing consumer base.

CONCLUSION

As a doctoral candidate, I set out to investigate a problem facing corporate America – shortage of talented labor. A result of the aging of baby boomers and shrinking pool of talent at the executive level, corporations will soon be hard-pressed to find enough qualified employees to fill executive-level positions. In addition to labor shortage, the U.S. is also seeing changing demographics, with the talent pool expected to see an increase of 148 percent for Asians, 139 percent for Hispanics and 58 percent for African Americans (Meyers and Dreachslin 2007).

This labor shortage problem and the changing demographics together present an opportunity to fill the African American void in the executive suite, where African American men are the most underrepresented group. To fill that void, companies should develop effective talent-management programs and succession-planning processes. My research, culminating in this book, presented a solution of focusing on African American men in the succession-planning and talent-management process as a way to bridge the impending labor gap.

Peterson, Philpot, and O'Shaughnessy (2007) provide support to this thought process, noting that African American men are third in the pecking order of corporate structures, after white men and white women. Hammett's concept of "Mini-Me-ism" about favoritism and politics within the organization, and other theories such as upper echelon theory and mirror-image hiring, all point to the common behavior of white managers choosing employees who look like him, passing over minorities who struggle to ascend in the organization. If organizations shifted their focus in talent management and succession planning to African Americans, a previously untapped talent pool of candidates can provide *Fortune 1000* companies the leaders they need to fill the vacancies that will soon be left by retiring baby boomers.

To shed light on the process of achieving success, I interviewed ten successful African American men who had experienced with talent-management programs and the succession-planning process, and had made their way into the executive suite. None of the executives I interviewed was looking for handouts, and none of them complained about being treated unfairly. None of the participants mentioned affirmative action as a reason for their success or as a badge to hide behind. They all indicated performance and competence as the keys to success within an organization. They pursued their career with a relentless resolve, focused on the prize of the executive suite, and undistracted from the setbacks in their journey such as being passed over for a promotion, the lack of organizational diversity or the non-exposure to training programs. They recognized the genuine trials and disappointments that they had to wrestle with, but they did not allow these roadblocks to derail them from their journey.

I also hope that the message of this book would capture the attention of *Fortune* 1000 leaders to change the way talent-management and succession-planning programs are administrated within their organizations for African

American men. For change to effectively occur the change has to transpire at all levels of organizational leadership and not just be relegated to human resource managers.

I also hope, of course, that African American men who aspire to attain senior-level positions will benefit from the message of this book. The executives shared their successes and failures, in order for the next generation of African American men to understand the process of gaining advancement in an organization. By sharing their tips and advice, and the 7 steps to success "PINDOWN," the executives' hope – and mine – is that other African American men would be empowered by this knowledge to press forward in their own individual journeys.

Brothers on the same journey, realize that no man is an island – you are not struggling alone. There are others who have run the race – they can show you the way. There are also others who are running the same race you are – reach out to them and encourage one another. There are still more who will follow you in your footstep – be their mentor and show them that success *is* possible.

REFERENCES

Allen, T. D., Eby, L. T., Douthitt, S. S., & Noble, C. L. (2002). Applicant gender and family structure: Effects on perceived relocation commitment and spouse resistance. *Sex Roles, 47*(11), 543-552. Retrieved from http://search.proquest.com/docview/225374603?accountid= 27965

Altman, W. (2009). Who's next in line? *Engineering & Technology, 4*(15), 72-75. doi:10.1049/et.2009.1516

Barnett, R., & Davis, S. (2008). Creating greater success in succession planning. *Advances In Developing Human Resources, 10*(5), 721-739. doi:10.1177/1523422308322277

Barney, S.M. (2002). The inclusive, diverse workplace: We are not there yet. *Journal of Healthcare Management, 47*(6), 356-369. Retrieved from http://search.proquest.com/docview/206724833?accountid= 27965

Brass, M. & Haggard, P. (2010). The hidden side of intentional action: The role of the anterior insular cortex. *Brain Structure and Function, 214*(5-6), 603-610. doi:10.1007/s00429-010-0269-6

Bell, J., & Hartmann, D. (2007). Diversity in everyday discourse: The cultural ambiguities and consequences of happy talk. *American Sociological Review, 72*(6), 895-914. Retrieved from http://search.proquest.com/docview /218826661?accountid=27965

Berchelman, K. D. (2005). Succession planning. *The Journal for Quality and Participation, 28*(3), 11-12.

Retrieved from http://search.proquest.com/docview/ 219119331?accountid=27965

Boatright-Horowitz, S., & Soeung, S. (2009). Teaching white privilege to White students can mean saying good- bye to positive student evaluations. *American Psychologist, 64*(6), 574-575. doi:10.1037/a0016593.

Brown, G. (2008) *African-American students defy the achievement gap: A phenomenological study.* (Doctoral dissertation). Retrieved from http://search.proquest.com/docview/304380629?accountid= 27965

Bureau of Labor and Statistics. (n.d.). *Electronic references.* Retrieved from http//www.bls.gov

Buttner, E.H., Lowe, K. B., & Billings-Harris, L. (2006). The influence of organizational diversity orientation and leader attitude on diversity activities. *Journal of Managerial Issues, 18*(3), 356-371,298. Retrieved from http://search.proquest.com/docview/194164928?accountid= 27965

Buttner, E., Lowe, K., & Billings-Harris, L. (2007). Impact of leader racial attitude on ratings of causes and solutions for an employee of color shortage. *Journal of Business Ethics, 73*(2), 129-144. doi:10.1007/s10551-006-9178-2

Byrnes, N., Crockett, R.O., & McGregor, J. (2009). An historic succession at Xerox. *Business Week*, (4134), 18-22. Retrieved from http://search.proquest.com/docview/236756982?accountid= 27965;magazine/content/09_23/b4134018712853.htm?cha n=magazine+channel_top+stories

Calo, T. J. (2008). Talent management in the era of the aging workforce: The critical role of knowledge transfer. *Public Personnel Management, 37*(4), 403-416.

Cantrell, S., & Benton, J.M. (2007). The five essential practices of a talent multiplier. *Business Strategy Series 8*(5), 358-364. doi:10.1108/17515630710684475

Cartwright, T. (2008). In focus/Getting results: The leadership value of setting priorities. *Leadership In Action, 27*(6), 18-21.

Cingoranelli, D. (2009). A 2009 tuneup your firm's succession planning. *Journal of Accountancy, 207*(3), 12, 42-46. Retrieved from http://search.proquest.com/docview/206798536?accountid=27965

Chanmugam, A. (2009). A qualitative study of school social workers' clinical and professional relationships when reporting child maltreatment. *Children & Schools, 31*(3), 145-161. Retrieved from http://search.proquest.com/docview/210949565?accountid=27965

Chee Sing, C., & Chia, E. (2009). State of the CIO 2009. *Enterprise Innovation, 5*(1), 14-16.

Cheese, P. (2008). Talent: A critical issue facing. *The British Journal of Administrative Management*, p.18. Retrieved from http://search.proquest.com/docview/224612324?accountid=27965

Comte, T. E. & Mihal, W. L. (1990). CEO turnover: Cause and interpretations. *Business Horizons, 33*(4), 47-51.

Cullinan, C. (2008). What types of companies choose CEOs with a marketing background? *The Business Review, 11*(1), 195-200. Retrieved from http://search.proquest.com/docview/197297621?accountid= 27965

Creswell, J., Hanson, W., Plano Clark, V., & Morales, A. (2007). Qualitative Research Designs: Selection and Implementation. *Counseling Psychologist, 35*(2), 236-264. doi.org.library.capella.edu/10.1177/0011000006287390.

Crescentini, A. & Mainardi, G. (2009). Qualitative research articles: Guidelines suggestions and needs. *Journal of Workplace Learning, 21*(5), 431-439. doi:10.1108/13665620910966820

Dalton, D.R. & Dalton, C.M. (2007). CEO succession: Some finer and perhaps provocative points. *The Journal of Business Strategy, 28*(3), 6-8. doi:10.1108/02756660710746300

Davidson, W., Ning, Y., Rakowski, D., & Elsaid, E. (2008). The antecedents of simultaneous appointments to CEO and Chair. *Journal of Management & Governance, 12*(4), 381-401. doi:10.1007/s10997-008-9066-5

Deeter-Schmelz, D., Goebel, D., & Norman, K. (2008). What are the characteristics of an effective sales manager? An exploratory study comparing salesperson and sales manager perspectives. *Journal of Personal Selling & Sales Management, 28*(1), 7-20.

Delmar, D. (2003). The rise of the CSO. *Journal of Business Strategy, 24*(2), 8. Retrieved from http://search.proquest.com/docview/202724591?accountid= 27965

Douglas, P. (2008). Affinity groups: Catalyst for inclusive organizations. *Employment Relations Today (Wiley), 34*(4), 11-18. doi:10.1002/ert.20171

Dowsett, C. (2007). How good companies go bad. *Strategic Finance, 89*(5), 15, 17. Retrieved from http://search.proquest.com/docview/229805708?accountid= 27965

Dutton, G. (2009) Succession success. *Training, 46*(4), 44-45. Retrieved from http://search.proquest.com/docview/203399102?accountid= 27965

Fairfax, L. (2005). Some reflections on the diversity of corporate boards: Women, people of color, and the unique issues associated with women of color. *St. John's Law Review, 79*(4), 1105-1120. Retrieved from http://search.proquest.com/docview/216774872?accountid= 27965

Fay, E. & Riot, P. (2007). Phenomenological approaches to work, life and responsibility. *Society and Business Review, 2*(2), 145-152. doi:10.1108/17465680710757367

Friedman, S.D. (1986). Succession systems in large corporations: Characteristics and correlates of performance. *Human Resource Management, 25*, 191-213. Retrieved from http://search.proquest.com/docview/224345377?accountid= 27965

Garrow, V. & Hirsh, W. (2008). Talent management: Issues of focus and fit. *Public Personnel Management, 37*(4), 389-402. Retrieved from http://search.proquest. com/docview/215948834?accountid=27965

Giorgi, A. (2008). Concerning a serious misunderstanding of the essence of the phenomenological method in psychology. *Journal of Phenomenological Psychology, 39*(1), 33-58. doi: 10.1163/156916208X311610.

Gilley, A., Gilley, J., & McMillian, H. (2009). Organizational change: Motivation, communication, and leadership effectiveness. *Performance Improvement Quarterly, 21*(4), 75-94. Retrieved from http://search.proquest.com/docview/218517376?accountid= 27965

Greer, C. & Virick, M. (2008). Diverse succession planning: Lessons from the industry leaders. *Human Resource Management, 47*(2), 351-367. doi:10.1002/hrm.20216

Guthridge, M., Komm, A., & Lawson, E. (2008). Making talent a strategic priority. *McKinsey Quarterly*, (1), 48-59.

Hambrick, D. C., & Mason, P. A. (1984). Upper echelons: The organization as a reflection of its top managers. *Academy of Management Review, 9*(2), 193–206. doi:10.5465/AMR.1984.4277628.

Hammett, P. (2008). The paradox of gifted leadership: Developing the generation of leaders. *Industrial and Commercial Training, 40*(1), 3-9. doi:10.1108/00197850810841585

Harlos, K.P., Mallon, M., Stablein, R. & Jones, C. (2003). Teaching qualitative methods in management classrooms. *Journal of Management Education, 27*(3), 304. Retrieved from http://search.proquest.com/docview/195701750?accountid= 27965

Hargreaves, A., & Fink, D. (2003). Sustaining Leadership. *Phi Delta Kappan, 84*(9), 693-700.

Hargreaves, A. (2005). Leadership Succession. *The Educational Forum, 69*(2), 163-173. Retrieved from http://search.proquest.com/docview/220687665? accountid=27965

Hastings, R. (2008, December). Obama election a boost for diversity. *HRMagazine,53*(12), 23-23. Retrieved from http://search.proquest.com/docview/205074306?accountid= 27965

Helfat, C., Harris, D., & Wolfson, P. (2006). The pipeline to the top: Women and men in the top executive ranks of U.S. corporations. *Academy of Management Perspectives, 20*(4), 42-64. doi:10.5465/AMP.2006.23270306.

Hite, L.M. (2006). Perceptions of racism and illusions of equity. *Gender in Management, 21*(3), 211-223. doi:10.1108/09649420610657399

Horner, S. (2009). Board power, CEO appointments, and CEO duality. *Academy of Strategic Management. Proceedings, 8*(1), 25-30. Retrieved from http://search.proquest.com/docview/192411567?accountid= 27965

James, V. (2009). Diversity quotas will be pain for firms. *Personnel Today*, 9. Retrieved from http://search.proquest.com/docview/229895110?accountid= 27965

Jones, N., & Wofford, J. (1983). 1999-The year of the Black CEO. *Business Horizons, 26*(3), 51.

Kalev, A., Kelly, E., & Dobbin, F. (2006). Best practices or best guesses? Assessing the efficacy of corporate affirmative action and diversity policies. *American Sociological Review, 71*(4), 589-617. Retrieved from http://search.proquest.com.library.capella.edu/docview/218 801550?accountid=27965

Kay, A., Gaucher, D., Peach, J., Laurin, K., Friesen, J., & Zanna, M., (2009). Inequality, discrimination, and the power of the status quo: Direct evidence for a motivation to see the way things are as the way they should be. *Journal of Personality & Social Psychology, 97*(3), 421-434. doi: 10.1037/a0015997

Kearney, E. Gebert, D & Voelpel, S. (2009). When and how diversity benefits teams: The importance of team members' need for cognition. *Academy of Management Journal, 52*(3), 581-598. doi:10.5465/AMJ.2009.41331431.

Lee, R. M. & Esterhuizen, L. (2000). Computer software and qualitative analysis: Trends, issues and resources. *International Journal of Social Research Methodology, 3*(3), 231-243.

Longenecker, C. & Fink, L. (2008). Key criteria in twenty-first century management promotional decisions. *Career Development International, 13*(3), 241-251. doi:10.1108/13620430810870494

Madden, C. S. (1991). Marketers battle for mind share. *Baylor Business Review, 9*, 8-8. Retrieved from http://search.proquest.com/docview/201170670?accountid=27965

Martin, C.A. (2005). Racial diversity in professional selling: An empirical investigation of the differences in the perceptions and performance of African-American and

Caucasian salespeople. *The Journal of Business & Industrial Marketing, 20*(6), 285-296. doi: 10.1108/08858620510618129

Maxwell, J. A (1992). Understanding and validity in qualitative research. *Harvard Educational Review, 62*(3), 279. Retrieved from http://search.proquest.com /docview/212250067?accountid=27965

McDonald, K.S. & Hite, L. M. (1998). Exploring the glass ceiling: An exploration of gender differences in management-development experiences. *Journal of Management Education, 22*(2), 242-254.

McDermott, M., Levenson, A., & Newton, S. (2007). What coaching can and cannot do for your organization. *HR Human Resource Planning, 30*(2), 30-37.

McNamara, K., Watson, J., & Wittmeyer, C. (2009). The utilization of a succession plan to effectively change leadership and ownership in a small business enterprise. *Journal of American Academy of Business, 15*(1), 31-42. Retrieved from http://search.proquest.com/docview/222848109?accountid= 27965

McVittie, C., McKinlay, A., & Widdicombe, S. (2008). Organizational knowledge and discourse of diversity in employment. *Journal of Organizational Change Management, 21*(3), 348-366. doi:10.1108/09534810810874822

Medcof, J. (2007). CTO power. *Research Technology Management, 50*(4), 23-31.

Miller, D. & Desmarais, S. (2007). Developing your talent to the next level: Five best practices for leadership.

Organization Development, 25(3). 37-43. Retrieved from
http://search.proquest.com/docview/198040536?accountid=
27965

Morrison, J. L., Oladunjoye, G.T., & Rose, D. (2008).
Effects of gender of executive leadership in management
upon perceptions related to enhancing workforce diversity.
*Journal of American Academy of Business, Cambridge,
13*(1), 79-85. Retrieved from
http://search.proquest.com/docview/222849241?accountid=
27965

Meyers, V.L. & Dreachslin, J.L. (2007). Recruitment and
retention of a diverse workforce: Challenges and
opportunities. *Journal of Healthcare Management, 52* (5),
290-298. Retrieved from
http://search.proquest.com/docview/206729524?accountid=
27965

Nasir, N., McLaughlin, M., & Jones, A. (2009). What does
it mean to be African American? Constructions of race and
academic identity in an urban public high school. *American
Educational Research Journal, 46*(1), 73-114. doi:
10.3102/ 000283120832279

Nicholson, G., & Newton, C. (2010). The role of the board
of directors: Perceptions of managerial elites. *Journal of
Management and Organizations 16*(2), 204-218. Retrieved
from
http://search.proquest.com/docview/577590062?accountid=
27965

Niehuis, S. (2005). Helping White students explore White
privilege outside the classroom. *North American Journal of
Psychology, 7*(3), 481-492.

Owens, L. A., & Young, P. (2008). You're hired! The power of networking. *Journal Of Vocational Rehabilitation, 29*(1), 23-28.

Peterson, C., Philpot, J., & O'Shaughnessy, K. (2007). African-American diversity in the boardrooms of the US Fortune 500: Director presence, expertise and committee membership. *Corporate Governance: An International Review, 15*(4), 558-575. doi:10.1111/j.1467-8683.2007.00588.x.

Pitcher, P. & Smith, A.D. (2001). Top management team heterogeneity: Personality, power, and proxies. *Organization Science, 12*(1), 1-18. Retrieved from http://search.proquest.com/docview/213831471?accountid=27965

Ready, R.A. & Conger, J.A. (2003). Why leadership-development efforts fail. *MIT Sloan Management Review, 44*(3), 83-88. Retrieved from http://search.proquest.com /docview/224964196?accountid=27965

Reed, K., Srinivasan, N., & Doty, D. (2009). Adapting Human and Social Capital to Impact Performance: Some Empirical Findings from the U.S. Personal Banking Sector. *Journal of Managerial Issues, 21*(1), 36-57, 6-7. Retrieved from http://search.proquest.com/docview/194164986?accountid=27965

Reilly, P. (2008). Identifying the right course for talent management. *Public Personnel Management, 37*(4), 381-388. Retrieved from http://search.proquest.com/docview/215932498?accountid=27965

Rizq, R., & Target, M. (2008). The power of being seen: An interpretative phenomenological analysis of how

experienced counseling psychologists describe the meaning
and significance of personal therapy in clinical practice.
British Journal of Guidance & Counselling, 36(2), 131-
153. doi:10.1080/ 03069880801926418

Rudis, E. (2006) Succession planning for top management
remains a major issue for global companies. *Employment
Relations Today, 33*(3), 51-59. doi:10.1002 / ert.20118.

Sieber, J. (2004). Empirical research on research ethics.
Ethics & Behavior, 14(4), 397-412.
doi:10.1207/s15327019eb1404_9

Shin, K., Kim, M., & Chung, S. (2009). Methods and
strategies utilized in published qualitative research.
Qualitative Health Research, 19(6), 850.
doi:10.1177/1049732309335857

Singh, V. (2007). Ethnic diversity on top corporate boards:
A resource dependency perspective. *International Journal
of Human Resource Management, 18*(12), 2128-2146.
doi:10.1080/09585190701695275

Sullivan, S. E., Forret, M. L., & Mainiero, L. A. (2007). No
regrets? an investigation of the relationship between being
laid off and experiencing career regrets. *Journal of
Managerial Psychology, 22*(8), 787-804.
doi:10.1108/02683940710837723

Taylor, C., Taylor, J. & Stoller, J. (2009). The influence of
mentorship and role modeling on developing physician-
leaders: Views of aspiring and established physician
leaders. *Journal of General Internal Medicine, 24*(10)
1130-1134. doi: 10.1007/s11606-009-1091-9

Taylor, J. E. (2004). *The new frontier for Black men: A
shifting view of senior leaders in organizations.* (Doctoral

dissertation). Retrieved from http://search.proquest.com/
docview/305045282?accountid=27965

Thornbory, G & White, C. (2008). How to....be proactive.
Occupational Health 60(3), 26. Retrieved from
http://search.proquest.com/docview/207325997?accountid=
27965

The U.S. Equal Employment Opportunity Commission.
2007EEO-1 National Aggregate Report. Retrieved
November 15, 2009 from http://www.eeoc.gov/eeoc/
statistics/employment/jobpat-eeo1/2007/us/national.html

Thompsen, J. A. (2009) Groom leaders. *Leadership
Excellence, 26*(4), 15-16.

United States Department of Commerce (1999, September).
Minority population growth: 1995 to 2050, *Minority
Business Development Agency.* Retrieved from
http://www.mbda.gov/documents/mbdacolor.pdf

Vollhardt, C. (2005). Pfizer's prescription for the risky
business of executive transitions. *Journal of Organizational
Excellence, 25*(1), 3-15. doi: 10.1002/joe.20075

White, B. (2009). Addressing career success issues of
African Americans in the workplace: An undergraduate
business program intervention. *The Career Development
Quarterly, 58*(1), 71-76 doi:10.1002/j.2161-
0045.2009.tb00175.x

White, K. M. (2006). Better manage your human capital.
Nursing Management, 37(1), 16-19.

Wilbanks, L. (2011) Performance reviews. *IT Professional
Magazine 13*(1), 58-60.

doi:10.1109/MITP.2011.13

Williams, D.A. & Wade, K.C., (2007). The chief diversity officer. *CUPA-HR Journal, 58*(1), 38-48.

Wilson J. B., and Natale, S.M. (2001) Quantitative and qualitative research: An analysis. *International Journal of Value Based Management 14*(1), 1-10. Retrieved from http://search.proquest.com/docview/195803250?accountid= 27965

Zane, N. C., (2002). The glass ceiling is the floor my boss walks on: Leadership challenges in managing diversity. *The Journal of Applied Behavioral Science, 38*(3), 334-354. Retrieved from http://search.proquest.com/docview/ 236323220 ?accountid=27965

Zhang, Y. (2006). The presence of a separate COO/president and its impact on strategic change and CEO dismissal. *Strategic Management Journal, 27*(3), 283-300. doi:10.1002/smj.517.

Zorn, D. M. (2004). Here a chief, there a chief: The rise of the CFO in the American firm. *American Sociological Review 69*(3), 345-364.

Zula, K., & Chermack, T. (2008). *Development and initial validation of an instrument for human capital planning.* (Doctoral dissertation). Retrieved from http://search. proquest.com/docview/304836490?accountid=27965

AUTHOR BIOGRAPHY

For the past 25 years, Dr. Jonathan Roberts has successfully climbed the steps to the executive suite of several Fortune® 500 consumer packaged goods organizations. He has led a dynamic career geographically, living in every region of the United States, which has enhanced his diverse understanding of organizational structures and the changing marketplace.

Dr. Roberts has enjoyed immense success in the corporate environment, winning several awards for his leadership and goal attainment. Likewise, he has a proven track record of developing talent. He has been appointed several times as a corporate liaison to represent company interests with industry trade organizations. He has also been an active member in the communities he resided in, having served on the local boards of The United Negro College Fund and The National Urban League.

In 2012, Dr. Roberts earned his Doctorate of Philosophy in Organizational Leadership from Capella University. He has leveraged his experience and talents and christened Onyx Management Consulting where he is focused on improving organizations and individuals' leadership capabilities. He specializes in leadership and talent development, team building, mentoring, coaching, and diversity and inclusion training.

Dr. Roberts and his wife reside in Atlanta, Georgia. He also has two daughters and a grandson. He is an avid reader, enjoys playing golf and is an enthusiastic fantasy football player.

Dr. Roberts is accepting engagements and requests for organizational or personal training. You may reach him at Onyxmanagementconsulting.com or drjonathanroberts1@gmail.com.

Made in the USA
Middletown, DE
24 May 2015